2012 OFFENSIVE LINE COACHES HANDBOOK

FEATURING LECTURES FROM THE 2012 C.O.O.L. CLINIC

Edited by Earl Browning

www.coacheschoice.com

© 2012 Coaches Choice. All rights reserved. Printed in the United States.

> No part of this book may be reproduced, stored in a retrieval system, or transmitted, in any form or by any means, electronic, mechanical, photocopying, recording, or otherwise, without the prior permission of Coaches Choice.

ISBN: 978-1-60679-230-8

ISSN: 1945-1172

Telecoach, Inc. Transcription: Emmerson Browning, Kent Browning, and Tom Cheaney

Diagrams: John Rice

Book layout: Bean Creek Studio

Cover design: Bean Creek Studio

Front cover photo: © Chad Ryan/Cal Sport Media/ZUMA Press

Back cover photo: Ron Chenoy-US PRESSWIRE

Special thanks to John Widecan of the University of Cincinnati for taping the lectures.

Coaches Choice
P.O. Box 1828
Monterey, CA 93942
www.coaceschoice.com

Contents

Speaker	Team	Topic	Page
Paul Alexander	Cincinnati Bengals	The Coda: Techniques for Better Blocking, Better Coaching, and How to Use Your Hands in Pass Protection	5
Mike Bloomgren	Stanford University	The Power Play and How We Teach Double-Teams	23
Dan Dorazio	British Columbia Lions	Double-Under and Single-Under Blow Delivery and Run Blocking Techniques	30
Pat Flaherty	New York Giants	Combination Run and Pass Protection Techniques	34
Jim McNally	Cincinnati Bengals	Losing Ground, Tipping, A Gap Entries, and Blocking Tips	50
Dante Scarnecchia	New England Patriots	Pass Protection Drills and Techniques	61
Mike Solari	San Francisco 49ers	Developing the Run Game With Fundamentals and Drills	69
Bob Wylie	Oakland Raiders	The First Meeting With Your Unit: Laying the Groundwork for a Successful Season	79
George Yarno	Detroit Lions	Five- and Six-Man Protection Techniques and Drills	89
About the Editor			103

Paul Alexander

THE CODA: TECHNIQUES FOR BETTER BLOCKING, BETTER COACHING, AND HOW TO USE YOUR HANDS IN PASS PROTECTION

Cincinnati Bengals

Here we go. This is the coda. What is a coda? In music, the term coda is the ending. It is the ending. The last time I talked here, the lecture was the prequel. The guys who were not here then have no idea what I am talking about. Today, I am going to talk to the people who have been with us on the topics. This is kind of the ending of that clinic. We were only halfway through the lecture the last session. I am going to talk about some of those things, and we are going to have some fun here.

I need to say this. I was trained as a teacher. I attended SUNY Cortland, which is an outstanding teachers college. I was trained as a teacher, and my background in teaching was in science. That is how I tend to think in terms of blocking. I see myself more as a scientist than a coach.

I also have an interest in music, and other ideas that relate to my background. Some of you may think it is weird that I am going to talk about playing the piano. Yes, I am going to talk about playing the piano. Talking about playing the piano in front of people is like performing in the NFL. The piano does not hit back. So I am going to talk about some of those weird things.

Here it is. I started with Albert Mühlböck, a world famous concert pianist. He was teaching my daughter. While I was watching him teach, I was thinking, *The man cannot speak English very well, but he would be a great football coach.* So I started taking piano lessons with him. I have learned all kinds of things about performing on a big stage, and overcoming those things. I am not going to get too theoretical on anything. I am going to talk very common sense and plain speaking terms.

I do want to play a short film. It will only last a couple of minutes. I am halfway embarrassed by it because there are a couple of points that are not necessarily true. Last summer, Albert Mühlböck and I went to Carnegie Hall, and Steinway Hall in New York, and all that kind of stuff. The NFL Films came in and filmed us. They made a segment that is kind of a lead-in to what all of this lecture is going to be about. I am going to play that for you, and I hope you enjoy it.

FILM

Paul Alexander

I think coaching and teaching is in the same line. I do not find inspiration always through football. I find it everywhere. After a long day with a million things on my mind, I play the piano and relax. Some guys work out, some guys play golf, and some guys read newspapers. I play the piano.

The journey started four years ago. I have a daughter named Carolyn. Carolyn is a very talented musician. She started learning to play the piano at the [College-]Conservatory [of Music] in Cincinnati under Albert Mühlböck. I look up Albert Mühlböck on Google. I found he has played the piano all over the world. He is a concert pianist. He was teaching my fourth grade daughter to play the piano.

A concert pianist is a great performer. I decided to learn to play the piano. I wanted to learn to play the piano for one reason, and that was to become a better football coach.

Bobbie Williams—Bengals, Guard

A concert pianist has similarities to playing a game of football. You are on this grand stage with everyone. If you mess up, there is no hiding from anyone. It is like playing the game of football. You are on national television with millions and millions of people watching. If you mess up, you can't take it back. You are on that stage.

Paul Alexander

When our guys break the huddle, they clap their hands and go up to the line of scrimmage. The most important thing they do is to keep their composure and their poise. It is no difference than being on the stage to play the piano. You go out on the stage and if you look at the audience and worry if they are going to like your music, you are going to fail. If you go on the stage and realize it is you and the piano, and that is all, if you can do that, you will be fine.

I have told a lot of people that Albert did not know anything about football. However, I have told them he would be a terrific football coach.

A part of coaching is getting the perfect feedback. I learned something from Albert Mühlböck through his training. It is a technique called the Alexander Technique. It is no relation.

You have seen violin players up tight and very stiff with the stroke and have difficulty getting the music correct. When you see them with the arms relaxed and the bow flowing smoothly across the violin, they do much better. The flow is smooth across the strings of the violin.

Andrew Whitworth—Bengals, Tackle

Coach Alexander is a unique guy. He believes in fine-tuning your game. For an offensive lineman, it is just like playing the piano. Technique is everything.

Man's mind once stretched by a new idea never regains its original dimensions.
—Oliver Wendell Holmes

Paul Alexander

I wrote a book by the title of *Perform*. Why did I write this book? I have never really believed in stereotype, and I have never believed that football players were dumb jocks. I never believed that musicians were a bunch of softies. I believe that people are people. There is something to be gained through everyone, and through everyone's accomplishment.

Albert Mühlböck—Concert Pianist

What I admire in Paul the most is in the fact he can connect this to feelings. He tells me what he used from our sessions he uses in coaching, and I find that exciting.

Bobbie Williams

He is always open to learn new ways. You have to respect that from a man that has been coaching in the NFL 20 plus years. He is still open to new ideas.

Andrew Whitworth

He seeks greatness for us in everything we do. That is his passion. If you are going to do something, be great at it. There are a lot of hobbies we like to do, and we want to be great at them. He wants to be in good in everything. He coaches the same way. He does not want you to be a good football player. He wants you to be a great football player.

Paul Alexander

I think we are put in this life with skills and gifts. I think it is our responsibility to hone those skills and gifts and to make the best out of them as we can. When someone does that, it is a wonderful moment.

I want to point out a couple of things from the film. *If you want to play loud, don't use force. More power comes from relaxed muscles than clinched teeth.* I know that. We will talk about that point. You can see something else in the film. We were moving around as we did the drills. I was walking around, and I threw something. What did I throw? I threw a can of spray paint. I coach with a can of spray paint a lot of the time. I spray the paint on the grass. I do it to teach younger players. I spray the paint where the player should step on a play. I spray the paint and have them place their feet on the paint marks on the grass. I do this often.

Here is the Alexander Technique that was talked about in the film. I taught Bobbie Williams that very technique. We were out on the practice field on a Friday. I had Andrew Whitworth stand across from him, pretending he had a rope tied to Bobbie Williams left knee. Bobbie Williams always had a hard time on cutting off defenders. He is a big, powerful-type player. He is one of the top run blockers in the NFL. He was always struggling with the cutoff block. The harder he tried to step, the worse he would do. He had to learn to completely relax. Stay with me on this. Instead of taking your body and moving your foot, you have an image that something is pulling your foot. It is completely different. If we are going to step in any direction, it is like a force of the rope pulling you to move. It is not like taking a "uh, step." When you "uh, step" you have tight muscles. In the Alexander Technique, you have the image that something else is moving you.

I developed a theory. I call it "tensed relaxation." I think this is true for all sports. We all have heard coaches say to players, "You are too tight. You need to loosen up. Come on, you have to be more intense." It is a Jekyll-and-Hyde thing constantly. "Come on, loosen up. Come on, let's go."

There is tension, and there is relaxation in every physical movement. If I am a baseball pitcher I have tension at two points. One is with the foot on the rubber, and the second is with my grip on the ball. Those are the two pressure points for the pitcher. The rest of the body is a whip, and it accelerates through the relation of the body.

Two years ago, I used the analogy of the Golden Gate Bridge. The reason the bridge stays up is because the edges are stressed against the banks. The arcing shape is what causes the structure of the bridge. It is the same for tense relaxation. If I am a blocker, my two tension points are my feet and my hands, and maybe my head if it is a three-point contact. The rest of my body is a whip into the block. It is not tight, and it is not stiff.

When they say a player is stiff, a lot of the times the player does not use his hips properly. I train this by getting the players to completely relax. A lot of times in dealing with big lineman, I tell them to relax. It is weird for a coach to be telling their players to relax, but it is true. "More power comes from relaxed muscles than from clinched teeth."

Let me talk about audiences. How do you get up in front of a crowd and play? I need a volunteer to assist me. Could I get someone to come up just for a second? "Thank you, coach. Would you stand up and sing 'The Star Spangled Banner' for us?" "I can't do that! I am not very good at that." OK! This is my point.

How do you get up in front of a crowd and perform? The first time I had to play a piano in front of people, my hands shook so bad I had to stop. I could not take it. I started thinking, *I am an NFL coach, and I am in front of millions of people.* I have faced the public most of my life. That is my job. I do not get nervous in coaching football.

But in doing something you are not used to doing, you do get nervous. It is true with something you do not feel good at doing.

There are some animals that get so nervous they faint. That is where we see the famous Tennessee Fainting Goat. They get so stressed out that they faint. It is called myotonia congenita. Their muscles get so locked up, and down they go. This is true.

The question is how do we get players to relax and to perform? Following is one thing to do. I was sitting at a Cincinnati Reds baseball game. I had the Diamond Seat closest to home plate. I have never been offered that opportunity again. This was over 10 years ago. I was close to the home plate, and I could see the faces of the batters. I looked at each player's face as he came up to bat. The look on the face of a Major League player at bat is amazing. The focus they have in their face and the concentration they have is unbelievable.

I did the same thing in 101 pass pro. I could stand over on the defensive side of the ball, and I could look at the focus the receivers have in their eyes and tell if they were good competitors or not. Players who have a lot of movement in the upper body have to learn to control it. They must learn to do that, and they must go beyond this point.

Following are some random thoughts on techniques. The left tackle lines up in our huddle so he can see the defensive personnel. He identifies the defense from our huddle, and he faces toward the line of scrimmage. That is his job. So much of our protection is based on what is initially seen from the defense. "Is the defense in the nickel, dime, or base? Is it heavy, 4-4 linebackers, or whatever?" Our left tackle's job in the huddle is to look at the defense. We have a trigger for him to look for. "When the noseguard (67) goes out of the game, it is a nickel or a dime defense." Our tackle watches the defensive alignment from the huddle, and he calls out the defensive personnel who are in the game.

We had a new coach on the staff this year, and he had never heard of teams doing this. He came from a very successful team, and he said he had never heard of the tackle looking at the defensive alignment from the huddle. So our left tackle calls out the defensive alignment before we break the huddle. We are aware of what we have to deal with from the defense before we break the huddle.

This photo is of this little character that I call solid hands (Diagram #1). Two years ago, I talked about this. When you hit someone with your hand, you do not slap it. You do not slap your hand at someone. Blockers learn to block with solid hands. I have the picture hanging up in the front of the room. I want them to think of solid hands when they are blocking. Most of this lecture is going to be about how you use your hands in pass protection. The big point I want you to get is the solid controlled hand on the blocker.

We do not punch with our fists. Everything is boom! If the defender tries to get around me, I use a club technique. The club technique is boom! I use the hand in the direction the defender is trying to get around me. It is a solid hand. Everything is a solid, controlled move with the hands.

Diagram #1. Solid Hands

It is just like an NBA basketball player dribbling the basketball. Watch how he dribbles the ball. He has big hands on the ball. When an NFL football player puts his hands on another player, it is solid hands.

Next, I want to talk about a new subject. I have never talked about this before. It is the capture technique. We kind of discovered this technique. It is used against fast linebackers that you need to lead on outside plays.

Say we are running an outside zone play, and our center has to block a very fast linebacker. The center knows he has to run like hell to get that linebacker. Also, the linebacker is a pain in the ass because he jumps around on you. If the center slows down just for a moment to make sure the linebacker is going outside, he can't get to the linebacker. That is a dilemma. How do you solve that dilemma?

This is what we decided to do. We told the center to go get that linebacker on a fast pace. If the linebacker hangs back, capture him with one hand. You do not have to put two hands on the fast-flow linebacker. Just put one hand on the linebacker. That gives the center confidence that he can control the linebacker with one hand. We call that the capture.

If the linebacker goes around the block, we use an old Tiger Johnson term. The center walks around the defender with his inside hand to block the defender. This is what the capture looks like (Diagram #2). It is an outside play, and the ball is going outside.

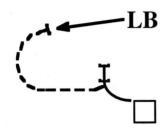

Diagram #2. Capture

The problem is if the center stops on the block, the linebacker overruns you. So you have to keep running. The problem is when the center keeps running, and the linebacker undercuts you, and he tries to hit him with two hands, he misses. The one-hand capture allows you to take care of that run-through linebacker on a fast-flow type of defender.

CAB PLAY/TAB PLAY

We are running an outside zone play or a mid-zone play to the tight end. You are worried about the noseguard slanting to the backside. We zone block with the center and the fullback (Diagram #3). It is a terrific thing. The fullback cuts the noseguard. It can be a wonderful way to slow that big fellow down.

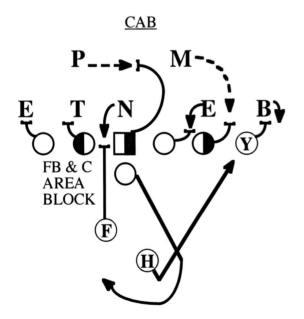

Diagram #3. Cab Play

We are manning the backside. We are expanding the backside to get the defense to stay put. We are not zoning it. We are stretching the frontside. We are putting the center out on his own. This is not a good deal. He is not really on his own because he and the fullback are going to work together. If the nose slants to the backside, the fullback is going to cut him.

There is a monster hole on this play. For four or five years, this has been our best average running play. We get a stretch on the frontside and backside of the ball at the line of scrimmage. Against the 3-4 defense in particular, it is a deadly play.

Against the Mike/Sam fire zone defense, that everyone hates, we have a problem. If you try to run a zone play to the tight end against a Mike/Sam fire zone, you are going to have problems. How do you handle the nose coming back on the play? This is the way to do it. Does the guard go all the way back?

We also run the play with the tackle and the fullback working together. We are running a weakside stretch play with the fullback leading to the weakside (Diagram #4).

Diagram #4. Tab

Let's say the defense is playing an over alignment. The guard has to work with the center on the nose man to the Mike linebacker, right?

Let's say the defense is playing an under alignment. The guard has to reach the 3 technique. The tackle rarely has help to the weakside on a mid- or outside zone play out of a two-backs set. So we put the tackle and back together in a tandem. It is a tackle and back technique: tab!

We do not like to use the technique on the inside zone play, but we do use it on the mid-zone or outside zone play. You run a lot of weakside zone plays, and what happens? The defense starts pinching the end inside to follow the back. If the defense pinches the end, and we have a tab scheme on, it is a 15-yard gain on the play every time. This gives the tackle confidence to make the play.

I thought Bob Wylie's lecture earlier tonight was wonderful. In the lecture, he used a term from a book by John Wooden. It is the term used in the pyramid that Coach Wooden wrote about. In the top block of the pyramid, the term "competitive greatness" is used. *Competitive greatness!* Educators watched John Wooden for a long time. They studied the type of feedback he gave his players. This is information used to train a teacher. This is what you learn when you study to be a teacher.

In studying the feedback from Coach Wooden to his players, they found he used three positives for one negative comment in the feedback to the players. It was almost psychical that a coach would be in a trend of three positive comments to one negative comment.

Am I telling you that everything should be positive? Hell, no! My young daughter's soccer team stomped the other team 12-1 early in the season. As I was walking by the other team, I heard one of the grandmothers say to one of the little girls, "Gee, it was not a very good game." The little girl responded, "At least we scored a goal!" The grandmother said, "Yes. That was great." I was thinking, *There is nothing positive about losing by a score of 12-1.*

I am not saying everything should be positive or negative. That is not my point. I was lucky to have coached for Bo Schembechler in 1986. In 1985, he had a 50 percent record. He never had a losing record at Michigan. He never had a losing record at Miami. He never had a losing record, but they were .500. We were in spring practice one day, and the assistant coaches had been on Bo about not being positive with the kids. "You have to be more positive with this type of play today."

That day, we were having a terrible practice. He called the team up all together. He said, "Men, my assistant coaches tell me I need to be more positive. I am positive! I am positive that we are horseshit. I know that. Let's start it over again."

The experts found that some teachers are more positive, and some are more negative. This is what they learned from Coach Wooden. You can tell a guy, "Good job." You can say, "Good job. I like how you set your feet before the pick." Here is the moment. You have been trying to get this player to do something forever. Finally, he gets it. You find yourself saying, "Great!" You could have gotten a junior high school or any other coach to say that. Your job as a coach is to seize that moment to say, "Great! Do you know why you got it? It was because of this or that."

I really believe this is important. I catch myself all of the time on this. I tell a player, "Good job," and then I pause and tell them why it is a good job or why it was a bad job.

Players coming to me today do not know how to cut block. They used to learn this in high school. It has changed today. Players do not know how to run block out of a three-point stance. We have to teach them how to run block out of a three-point stance. And we have to teach them how to cut block.

CUT DRILL

We have a drill we teach the players now, and we call it our "cut drill." The first time they did the drill, it was awful. The blocker goes past the man he is responsible for. When he cuts, he lunges; he accelerates his feet all the way through the block, arches the hips, and accelerates the body. The block can happen for down linemen, it can happen on screens, and it can happen on whatever. I am determined, once a week, to teach the drill for cut blocking. It is a lost art. It used to be that anyone coming out of high school could cut block. I find this is not true sometimes.

FALLBACK DRILL

You are blocking someone on an outside play, and as you are blocking the man, he falls back. We use the term "falling back," meaning the back cuts up, and the defender comes off your block and makes the tackle. Maybe the back cut up too soon. You still must block the man who fell off your block. Are you with me? I am blocking this man, and we have an offensive running back with me. I have outside leverage on the defender. The man I am blocking comes off and makes the tackle. I am thinking the back is going to cut back behind my block, but he does not cut back, and my man makes the tackle. That is a problem. How do you block that defender?

This is what you do. You block the defender, and the important thing is this. You must be conscious of your inside hand. If I am blocking a defender, and he moves with my offensive back, and as I feel him move, I take my inside hand, and instead of being on his chest, I will replace the inside hand deep toward the back of the defender. After I get my inside hand around his side, as he starts to go back inside, I can block him because I have control of the defender with my inside hand. If the defender moves on me, then I get the inside hand deep. For the guys who know me, I do this clubbing and lifting in pass protection. It is kind of all and all the same.

EYE TARGETING

Covering vs. Target Focus

Do you put your eyes somewhere, or do you cover the defender in pass protection? I have now taught when I set on a pass block, I stare at a target. I do not teach the blocker to look at the inside number, or the inside armpit, or the head, or whatever you may teach. The reason is this: When you stare at a target, your body becomes tight and you become too focused.

What I really believe you do in pass protection is this: You cover the defender's angle with your body. I feel my body cylinder covering his body of rush. From there, I am going to put my eyes in specific places. I will talk about that later. It just dawned on me to ask the players if they focused on a different part of the body. I went around the meeting room, and I asked each player what they focused on during a pass block.

"When you pass block, do you look at a specific target, or do you just cover the pass rusher with your body?" Almost everyone in the room said, "I do not know. I just cover the man with my body. I do not really stare at anything particularly."

If the defender comes with an overhand move, the blocker cannot see it. He has to see more peripheries. He has to see what his hands do so I will know what my reaction is going to be. We always block the surface that is presented to me. I am not going to turn and set at a specified time. The defender's surface is going to tell me how to block that man. What he gives me is going to tell me how to block him.

We look somewhere from the naval to the chest area. We look at the torso, the part of the body that is connected. We never look at the head when we are eye targeting on pass blocking. However, we do have special targets. Any defender who has a great move, such as Reggie White had, is difficult to block. When he had the hump, he would come upfield and hump the blocker like crazy. He would kill the blockers. Anyone who has an explosive move like he had is difficult to block.

Watch what happens when you hump a blocker. I come toward the blocker. Before I hump, an equal and opposite reaction with the opposite arm has to happen. Then, I hump with the opposite arm. So when we blocked Reggie White, we looked at his outside hand. The reason for that was because his outside hand would show it first with the hump. If you waited to read the hump, you were humped.

If you are blocking against a player who has a great spin move, before the spin there has to be some type of opposite reaction. Are you with me? Before he spins, he has a reaction to go back the other way. Typically, it is the inside hand. When the inside hand goes up, here comes the spin. So if you are blocking against a defender who has a great spin move, you focus on his inside hand. The blocker does not stare at the same target for every single defender he blocks. They all have different moves.

The same thing is true with the feet. Some defenders are strictly circular rushers. They rush up and inside, or they are circular rushers. I tell our blockers to set and to look at the feet of the defender he is blocking. His feet may not be in rhythm. Some guys are simple in their rush. It is one, two, three, and go! You can time their move. You can see his move before it happens.

Here is what drives you crazy. This is a good thought. Typically, if I am a left tackle, and I am blocking the man to my outside, the defender is taught to line up with his outside foot back. Take three steps inside: left, right, left, and then inside.

There are some rushers, and I will not name them, but they are difficult to block.

Ten percent of the rushers in the NFL line up with their feet backward on the rush. They have the inside foot back. Now, the move is left, right, and then inside. If he goes left, right, left, then inside, it is too late. If you are blocking a defender who lines up in a backward stance, the move generally comes off sooner, because it comes off two steps instead of three steps. Now, when we block that defender, instead of taking two kick slides, which times up with a step, step, step move, we cut the slides down and only take one kick slide. We look for the quick inside move off two steps instead of three steps.

It is the same thing we do with defenders who have similar hand knockdowns. If a defender has an outside hand chop, I am going to find something on that film that tells me when that chop is coming. I am not going to wait for the move that happens. Any defender who has a great move has something that indicates his move. It may be a windup type of move before that move happens. When you find the key to the windup, you have stopped the defender's move.

There is only one bass in the orchestra! The bass is a musical instrument that makes a loud "bah" sound. This is not true. There is usually a half dozen. For our purpose here, we are saying there is only one. We had a problem with Andy Dalton when he first came to us. *Where is Coach Eddie Williamson? There you are! I want to thank you for sending Andy Dalton to us. He is terrific. He knows protections, and just about everything.*

When Andy Dalton gets in a loud stadium, you can't hear him. He has a very normal voice. His voice is similar to what my voice is right now. I coached for Coach Joe Paterno at Penn State. You could hear Joe Paterno anywhere on the field. He had an off-key tone to his voice, and you knew it was Joe when he talked. You could hear him anywhere.

We have Jonathan Hayes on our staff. He has a very deep, bass tone to his voice. "Hey, get your ass over here." The whole team can hear him. Why is it you can hear those guys? This is why!

When I was coaching with the New York Jets, we were playing Denver, and John Elway was their quarterback. It was late in the fourth quarter, and we were playing at the Meadowlands. We were winning late in the fourth quarter. Elway and Denver had the football. That was not a good deal. He won a lot of games late.

The crowd is going crazy. The crowd was so loud, you could not hear anything. The only thing I could hear on the sideline was, "Set, blue 88, blue 88." That was all I could hear. Great! The only thing they could hear was Elway's cadence. Do you know how those quarterbacks have a phony cadence? "Set, blue 16, blue 16." They do not talk like that in real life. Here is the problem. When you talk in frequencies that are in normal range, this is what happens. If we have everyone in the room talking at one time in a normal tone of voice, and I try to get their attention, they will not hear me.

Why did you hear your mother call out "Dinner" when you were outside? It is the same thing in our house. My wife yells at the kids. We have a family room with a tall, cathedral-type ceiling. Her voice will vibrate around the ceiling in the family room. I think to myself, *Why does it have to be that high and that loud?* The only saving grace we have is this, guys. As we get older, we hear less. This is particularly true of the higher pitched frequencies. I call this God's compassionate plan for the married man. That is what I call it.

I told Andy Dalton this same story in front of the whole team just before our first game because we could not hear him. I told him the story about John Elway. All of a sudden, two things happened. His register where his commands came from was lower. I had told him he could go lower or higher on his cadence. I instructed him not to be on the same frequency with everyone else.

I was a singer back in my early years. We learned how to apply pressure to the stomach and to force air from the stomach. It is the same thing as I teach in pass protection. The pressure is not from the throat. You force the air from the stomach. You teach how to apply pressure to the stomach to project your voice. Air, volume, power, and pitch make the voice so you can hear individuals.

When our center goes up to the line of scrimmage, this is what he says. "Mike, 5-2, hut." This is how our center communicates. The center does not go up to the line and call out "Mike, 5-2, hut" in a low tone of voice. Woody Hayes, the legendary coach at The Ohio State University, understood this concept. What were his line calls? Gap it, drive it, and dig it. Everything had the word "it" at the end of the description. He said he learned this when he was a naval officer in communication.

I think the same thing is true with the calls we make along the line of scrimmage. It is true with the quarterback or anyone else that communicates with the other team members about the depth and force of the pitch.

SCORE PERSPECTIVE

If you are losing the game in baseball, and it is the sixth inning, and the score is 3-1. This is no big deal, right? Even if the score is 4-1, it is no big deal. Why is it in football, it is the start of the fourth quarter and you are losing 28-7 or 21-7, and you say, "We are getting our ass kicked?" No, you are not getting kicked in the ass. When we get in a similar situation, I tell our players, "Look, we are only down two or three runs." We only have to score twice and we can make up the deficit. If you are down 14 points, you do not have to score 14 times. You have to score twice. It is a little bit of hope you can give your players in those situations.

Here is a photo of my teacher in piano, Albert Mühlböck. The hands of the pianist go up and down the keyboard so fast. They do it so fast because they practice so precise. They do not move their hands until they know exactly where the hands are going. You do not let your hands take over. I teach the same thing in blocking. Make your mind tell your feet to move in drills.

I am going to make my mind tell my right foot to move six inches right now! I talk about this in blocking. I do the same with my hands. I am going to put my hand at a certain spot on the defender now!

Willie Anderson was the best at this technique. Willie kind of taught me about having a solid core in breathing. We have worked on improving the breathing when blocking. It is something you must do. When you block, you breathe, but you are solid as you move.

Players have to learn to breathe from the diaphragm when they are blocking. For most players, when they breathe, their shoulders go up. You have to learn to keep the shoulders level and breathe from your diaphragm. Otherwise, you get yourself out of whack.

SLIDING BUT STAYING IN THE MIDDLE

This is something I believe in. We work a lot on slide protection. Everyone in football uses slide protection. If you are a West Coast offense, you call it two-jet, or jet protection. It can be what you want to call it. But it is when you are sliding to block on a Will linebacker. It can be a slide to the outside to Will, or it can be a slide inside to Will. Every team I see in those slide protections takes their center and slides him over to the man he is blocking. The right guard has his man by himself, and the tackle has his man by himself. On the other side of the line, we are 3-on-2 against the defense.

Here is what I am going to propose. If I were the center, and I knew the linebacker was not going to blitz, I would never leave the middle. I would never ask the lineman to cover a distance that far. It is too much space to cover. So when I know that linebacker is not blitzing, the center is setting in the middle. How do we know if the linebacker is blitzing or not? One way is by the depth of the linebacker.

Here is another way to tell if the linebacker is blitzing or not. If the linebacker has his hands on his knees, he is not blitzing. Check it out. Chart it. They never blitz when they have their hands on their knees. They are getting ready to cover. You can find different tips on each linebacker. When a linebacker is going to blitz, he has to move up on his toes and he drops his hands to the side. If the linebacker has his hands on his knees, then I am going to stay in the middle.

We find tips where the linebacker will show when he is going to blitz. If I know the linebacker is not blitzing, I am going to keep the center in the middle of the line. We want to keep the middle of the protection solid. Only when I am almost sure the center is going to blitz will I send the center outside to block the linebacker.

If the linebacker is deep, he is not in a good posture to blitz. It will take him longer to come on the blitz. If the linebacker is deeper, we have more time to get over to the area where he is blitzing.

I see teams that bring the linebacker outside, looking for the linebacker to blitz, and it is third down and 15 yards to go for a first down. The linebacker is playing very deep and is not going to blitz, and the center is leaving the middle, coming outside looking for the linebacker to blitz. The right guard is getting drilled inside. I just do not understand when teams do this.

Why would you want to leave the middle open? Sometimes, you may have to do it because you have a mismatch outside the tackle. But when things are equal, keep the center in the middle as much as you can.

Those who have heard me before have heard me talk about scarecrow coaching. Basically, the question is what do you do on the day before the game in the afternoon practice that day? The other players are working on four hours of returns, and you are over on the side working your butt off with the offensive line. The players want nothing to do with you as the coach. So the coach has to come up with some drills to kill that time slot.

For one drill we came up with, we have a little contest. We take a piece of tape about six inches and mark the spot where the front foot is before the snap. We have the lineman take two slide steps: set, one, two. Then, we place another piece of tape on the spot where the front foot is after the slides.

We have the same player go back to his original stance. I tell the player to close his eyes. I am into this kinesthetic awareness thing. He wants to move his body without counting on his eyes. Again, we call out, "Set, boom, boom." The player takes two slide steps. The good players can come down on that piece of tape on the second slide. The players who rely on their visual acuity can't step on that second piece of tape.

PASS PROTECTION TECHNIQUES AND TIDBITS

Let's talk about setting to the spot. Keep your eyes level. Where is Billy Best? This is a tip I got from him last year. This is very good. When you pass set, keep your eyes level. When some players pass set and slide along the line, they get a little erratic and move the head up and down. They get a little "hippity hoppity." This is what I got from Billy Best, and I love it. You want that sense that your eyes are level.

CONSTANT FOCUS

Too many blockers do this in pass protection. They focus as they take their stance, and then they slide and they lose their focus. Then they focus again. The focus must be constant throughout the stance, the kick, the slide, and the whole works. They must be bent, with good posture, and with focus all the way through the block.

GUARD SET

Where does the guard set? Does he set too deep? Did he set too flat? This is what I tell them. I set nose-to-nose. I do not set on the inside of a guard. You can't stop a 3 technique from rushing up the field that way. I get upset about this every time I lecture, because I know it to be true. I get nose-to-nose with the man. I will show how to recover if he goes inside. I go one, two, and kick slide.

If the man comes straight at the guard, he puts his hands up on the pads, and he is in perfect position. My fingertips are just about on the man, and that is a perfect relationship.

If I am a guard with extremely long arms, I could probably sit back a little more and still be okay. If the guard wants to know if he is too deep, all he has to do is to take the one, two slide steps, and if you are head-up with the defender, you are in good position. We talk about the fingertip relation.

I set the tackles on a 45-degree angle. The angle for the guard is 45 degrees. In reality, that is not right. The guard's angle on a wide 3 technique is more like a 30-degree angle. So I do this circuit drill every day. If you want to see my circuit drill, you can go to my website at: www.perform-coach.com, and you can see the drills. I have cones that are four yards apart I use in the drills. There are six of the cones. I got this drill from one of the Steelers coaches. The drill is based on the fact that you take two different angles or movements when you pass set. You either post laterally, or you kick at a 45-degree angle.

Next to the circuit drill, I have six other cones set up that are closer together. This setup is for the guards and center to force them to take a 30-degree angle movement.

GUARD SET ON A 3 TECHNIQUE

Our guard pats the leg of the center when we are ready for the snap on the shotgun. We do not have the center look back for the quarterback. This allows the center to make the line calls, and he never has to take his eyes off the defense.

Here is my theory: "Guards, if the 3 technique goes out, knock him outside." This is the rule other than against the four vertical. Nate Livings, my right guard, told me, "When I am out on the field, I hear your voice. I hear the same terms you keep telling us over and over again. I get ready to block a man, and I hear your voice. I hear the same things over and over again: feet before hands."

That is one of the techniques I use with players. It is called "brainwashing." "When the 3 technique goes outside, knock him out." There is nothing worse than the guard against a rusher staying on the 3 technique outside. Inevitably, what happens is a couple of things. As the guard stays with the 3 technique, the defensive end twists around on a tackle-end stunt and goes inside, and the guard can never get off the block on the 3 technique. The other thing that happens is the 3 technique grabs the guard when he is stuck on him. The 3 technique pulls the guard, and he can't get away.

I learned a long time ago if the defense is holding us, it was my job to do something about it so they don't hold us. It was better to come up with something to prevent the holding rather than complaining about the defensive man holding us. What I came up with is this: "When the 3 technique goes out, knock him out with a block and a side shuck." It is a block and a side shuck to knock him flat.

Think about it. If I just knock the 3 technique outside, and he resets his rush, we have nothing. No harm, no foul, right? At worse, when he comes back at me, I can grab him.

Here is a rule: Never punch twice. If I were to knock a defender out, then I could grab him. It is the only time I would punch the man. If he is off of me and I wanted to displace his momentum, I would grab him. If the man has no momentum, I would not punch him again. We have seen it before. You are the tackle, and you punch the rusher. All of a sudden, you punch him again, and he knocks your arm off the block, gets around you, and gets the quarterback. So we never punch twice. If we do, the second type punch is some type of a grab.

PHYSICAL MIDDLE

We want a physical middle. That is why we try to keep the center in the middle as much as possible. That is one of the reasons we do all of the hand movements that we do. We want our protection to be strong in the middle.

GO IN PEACE

I am Catholic, and this has something to do with my coaching. I was raised that way, and that is just how I am. I get to church early. I am a good Catholic, and I get to the church real early. I park in the first spot to get out of the parking lot when church is over. When you are Catholic, you go to church to do your sacraments, to fulfill your obligations, and to make your sacrifice, and then you get the hell out of there and watch football.

I married a Protestant. When her church service is over, they experience fellowship. They have coffee, and so forth.

We have a priest in our church. This is how the priest ends our service: "The Mass has ended. *Go in peace!*" I am trying to get out of the church. There is my wife. I have to drag her out. I tell her, "The priest said, Go in peace! He did not say stick around and talk." By the time we get to the parking lot, we are the only car left in the parking lot. I coach the same way.

You are the line coach, and you are standing next to your players throughout practice. Then, the head coach calls them up as a group. After a few comments, he breaks them. Then, I have to talk to them at the end of practice? Are you kidding me? If I had something more meaningful, I would have said it before the end of practice. I may be early getting on the practice field, but I assure you I am the first person off the practice field when that practice is over.

I do this with my players because I want them to have the mentality that we work until the whistle blows. Then, we go in because practice is over. So when our practice is over, we "go in peace."

BULL RUSH—LOW HANDS

How do you stop a defender who bull rushes you? I do principles of blocking that I call "teeter-tottering." The term *low hands* was invented by yours truly. As lineman, we always start with our hands up. In low hands, we move our hands low so they can move from low to high. There is a teeter-tottering principle. I have told the story that I invented the term when I was at my mother-in-law's house, and I watched her stupid bird moving its head back and forth like a teeter-totter. I finally learned how pass protection works.

When you punch out in pass protection, your body follows your hands. How many times have you heard a coach tell a blocker, "You lunged at him, you dropped your head, you overextended." You hear all of those words. I never say those words, because we never have our hands up high. We never overextend in pass protection. When I say never, I mean never. Every now and then, our center gets too jacked up on a guy and lunges at the defender. That drives me crazy.

When we punch with our hands and the hands go from low to high, it is an equal and opposite reaction. When the hands go up, the shoulders go back, and we do not lunge.

When a defender bull rushes you, you want the hands lower than his hands. Even if he gets his hands on me first, if he only exerts half speed on me, he can't move me because I have my hands lower than his hands. I have leverage on the defender. This is my point for the low hands.

We have all said, "The man who gets his hands on the opponent wins." No! That is an incomplete statement. This may be out and out fraud! What really happens is this: The man who has leverage on the other man in a bull rush wins. The rusher can put his hands on my shoulders, but if I have my hands on his chest, I win.

When he pushes on me, instead of stepping back, I do a sprawl technique that is used in wrestling. Only 10 percent of the players in college know how to do this because I work the players out. Howard Mudd calls the technique a flop. We have low hands, and I lift the man with my hands, and then I set my feet. Now, the defender cannot walk me back. Let the defender make the first move, most of the time. Don't reach for him.

How many times, with the way NFL Films look, do you actually punch with two hands straight out in front of the man? I have no evidence, but I would say it is around 10 percent of the time. Almost all pass protection hand techniques are done with one hand first, and then the second hand comes. The pass protection hand techniques are one, two. The only way to directly punch the defender is if he is directly in front of you, where you can hit him with both hands at the same time.

Look at all of our drills. All of our drills are two-hand punch drills. We do very few two-hand punch drills. I concentrate on training the hands for pass protection.

Does the blocker keep his back nice and straight to punch the rusher? Never! The NFL lineman cannot keep his back perfectly straight and punch out and try to stop the man. An NFL player must get a little momentum from somewhere to accomplish that block.

UPPER PUNCHING

On the upper punch, the left guard lifts with his arms as he makes contact with the defender. He lifts instead of punching.

TAKE CHEST

I am going to get into different reads that you take on a defender. First is with the defender coming straight at me. This is where I take his chest, I lift him, and I grab him. Block the surface that is presented to you. If the defender gives you the chest, take it with two hands underneath the chest area.

CONFIDENCE IS A DECISION

This is what I tell the players. It is like being on a high diving board. You either have to jump, or you have climb back down. When you play in the NFL, or you get up to sing the national anthem, you either do it, or you do not do it. "Confidence is a decision." I believe that is a true statement. You can talk yourself into about anything. How many of you guys have been married for 20 years? I told you that you can talk yourself into anything. You could have gotten rid of your wife a long time ago. You can talk yourself into anything, and you can make the decision to be confident.

Some of you think I deal with only great athletes. Also, I deal with some feeble, confident people. They have to go block a great defensive rush lineman. The offensive player may not have been drafted. You tell that player when he gets to the line to go block the defender.

BULL FLOP

Here is the Howard Mudd flop. It is the sprawl technique that I like to call it with the left guard: "low hands feet flop." Don't walk back with our feet. Ninety percent of the players coming out of college walk back with their feet. It is step left, right, left, right. They need to learn to retreat with two feet together.

I tell the linemen to think of their feet as tent stakes. The people from the North can understand this point. I am from the Rochester, New York, area. The coaches from Wisconsin can understand this point as well. Rochester is similar to Wisconsin, just on the other side of the lake. We all know that when we go camping, there is a law. First, you set up the tent, and then you start drinking—in that order. You never start drinking before the tent is set up. If they do not get the tent stakes in the ground at the proper angle, you will wake up in the morning, and the tent will be on your face. That does not do you any good.

It is the same in pass blocking protection. Think of your feet as tent stakes that will hold your body and prevent the wind from blowing you over.

THIRD PERSON

How about this point on building confidence? Working with great players, they believe there is a third person somewhere who works with them. It is true, as I know, having worked with great piano players and pro football players as well. Most of them talk in terms of a third person. However, most of them have enough smarts that they do not talk about this in public.

In the locker room, getting ready for the game, they get dressed. They put on their shoulder pads, and they get another player to help them put their jersey on. Then, for some reason, they have to go take a leak. Every one of them does it. On the way to the urinal, there is a mirror on the wall. They all walk up to the mirror and look at their face. They all seem to have a zit in a spot just above their upper lip. What are they doing there? That third person is coming out in them. So what you have to do is to harness that third person.

Some of you may say there is no such thing as the third person. Have you ever watched Peyton Manning after he throws an interception? As he leaves the field, he starts mumbling. He is talking to that third person.

Here is a new story. I am telling it for the first time. We are talking about the bull rush. The defender comes at me and hits me in the chest area. The blocker takes the chest. Next is when we set for the bull rush, and the defender attacks the right or outside arm. If the defender is head-up, or a couple of feet outside or inside, I know what to do. What I do not like is when the defender is just off the center of my body to one side or the other.

The question is: how to block that defender? Do I take two hands? Do I club the man? I can't do either. If the defender is taking an angle where he is attacking your hand, and it does not matter if it is the inside or the outside hand, we use a technique we call the "stab." As the defender comes forward, we take a stab at his chest and reset our feet. It is not a launch move; it is a stab and reset the feet. It is similar to a six-inch jab to the chest area.

Let me talk about the outside rush for a moment. For a part of the outside rush, there is a segue phase to it. Segue, meaning how do you get from here to there? Segue is the combination of footwork (pigeon toe), hands (double clamp), and angle (push). When I set to the defender, it is my transition to a point of finishing the block. The segue parts are pigeon toe, which means to set your inside foot so you can open at a good angle. It means don't just sit and chase. Set your inside foot, kick slide, pigeon toe so you can open on a good angle. It also has to do with the hands, the angle, and the push. When I take the defender around the tackle, I do not whirl him around. It is more like tether-balling the man around on the block. We set the foot, and we push on the defender.

If I am setting as a tackle, I want the inside foot straight to slide, but then at some point, as the defender makes his rush, you want to turn your foot so it is pointing outside at a 45-degree angle. I do this so I can open my hips and push outside on the defender. If I do not set my foot when the defender circle rushes me, then I will be behind the block, chasing from behind. Coach McNally would always say, "Helmet adjust properly for the guys." How do we properly helmet adjust? It is kick slide, pigeon toe, push.

SOMETIMES WE PUNCH

When do we punch? The only time we punch is when the defender is off our blocker. If a blocker sets, and the defender comes to the blocker, he is going to grab him in some manner. We are never going to do one of those slide drills where we slide down the line, punching the dummies as we move down the line. "Bam, slide, bam, slide, bam" We are not going to that. We do not do a drill like that. I do not see this in the NFL Films. I have seen it on practice fields. However, I do not see it on NFL Films. When I see NFL, everyone is "Bam," and sitting on the rusher in pass protection.

When do we punch? We punch when the defender is away from us, where we can't grab the man. It is like a wide circle rusher on a pass rush. We take the thumbs and cross them together. We pigeon toe, and we punch the tip of the shoulder with two hands to knock him off-balance because he is too far away from me. We do a two-hand punch at the tip of the shoulder. We never punch twice.

Willie Anderson played against Jevon Kearse. Willie was at Auburn University and played against Jevon, who was at the University of Florida. When the Tennessee Titans were in our division, they played against each other twice a year. I will say it honestly. Kearse, you know he was a "physical freak." He had a great body, with a slim waist, and a big upper body. At the end of his career, I asked Willie, "How come Kearse never beat you on a play." His reply was this: "I never looked at him." I said, "What do you mean, you never looked at him?" "I would break the huddle and go up to the line of scrimmage. I would look across the line to see where his feet were. But, I would never look at him for the entire game. I would drop to my spot, and I would block the guy, and I would go back to the huddle. I would never look at him."

I asked him why he never looked at Jevon. He replied, "He is a freak! If I looked at him, I would have made a mistake. I would have been going over all of the things I would have to do to block Jevon, so I never looked at him."

The point is this: Most pass rushers beat pass blockers with technical errors. Not many pass rushers can beat a blocker whose pass blocking technique is sound. It is because they do not have the geometry to get it done. They have to force it in some way.

I have one more Willie story. When he was a rookie, he played against Bruce Smith. Bruce Smith could really rush. He was amazing. Willie was playing against Bruce Smith when he was a rookie. Bruce Smith had 250 sacks at that time. It was a mismatch of huge proportion. When we were stretching before the game, I went up to Willie. I kneeled down in front of him and said, "Willie, relax. Bruce Smith is not going to kill you." Willie, a young guy, looked up and said, *"Really!"*

When you think of it that way, it helps. Are you with me? No one dies of spontaneous combustion in football. Do you know what I mean? You do think, "Oh, he is going to kill me." I have never seen that happen in the NFL. "Just get in front of the guy, and Willie, you are good. Take the right angle. Use your hands, Willie. You are good." You do not go back to the quarterback and tell him you are sorry. Don't let him hit the quarterback! Do you have it?

**THE CLUB AND BLOCKING
IN THE THIRD DIMENSION**

The club is a security blanket. Some people think it causes you to get holding penalties. We do not get holding called often. There is no rule that says I cannot extend my arm into the chest of a pass rusher. If he continues to rush upfield, I can keep my arm extended into his chest. That is legal. Use of the club techniques is not holding. I am punching the defender who is rushing in the chest, and I am sliding my feet as I move with him. This stops his rush.

Why do the tackles turn too soon? They turn too soon because they are afraid the defender is going to run by him. You set up square, and you have the security blanket so if someone runs outside on you, you use the club technique. We get our near hand on his chest, and we slide our feet with him as he continues upfield.

What we are trying to do is to block a defender forward, sideways, or even on an angle, or straight up. We never really talk about blockers. This is very important in talking about that third dimension, which is around and around. I talk about blockers as if they were spinning tops.

There are two theories. First, we see a Rip move. There is the one theory of catching the Rip and stopping it as the defender starts his move inside. That is a good theory. The other theory that I subscribe to is this: When the defender brings the Rip, we twist the near arm of the rusher and turn him in the direction he is going. We block him like a top.

If the defender rushes outside of me, I am going to grab him with my outside arm. On any move that is off the edge, there is a point in time when the feet of the defender are in a crossing position. The art in blocking a defender like a top is to time your momentum, so when the defender's feet come together, that is the time to twist the defender.

OUTSIDE KNOCKDOWN

We never set and punch on a defender. Never! If the defender tries to knock our outside hand down with his outside hand, we move it under his hand. We never put our hands up in front of our chest with our thumbs together in the middle of the chest. Think of your hands as the stagger of your feet. If my left foot is up, my left hand is up. The right hand is back because the right foot is back. My hands mirror the stagger of my feet.

We would never put our hands together with the fingers interlocked with our feet staggered. If we did that, my body would work in opposite frames.

In an outside knockdown move, our left tackle uses a wrestling technique against the rusher. When the defender starts his club move, I want to turn him like a spinning top.

BEAR CLAW

The bear claw was just invented last year. It is a good device. You can go to that website (www.madathletic.com), and you will find that I have 12 different blocking techniques that you can teach with the bear claw (Diagram #5).

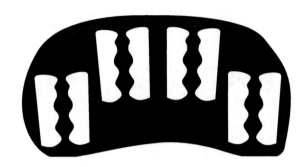

Diagram #5. Bear Claw

We use this drill every day as part of our circuit. This is where you teach the coordination of the hips and the hands. You start with the bear claw low, and bring it up to the height of the shoulders. Also, we do a push-pull drill with the bear claw. We do all kinds of drills with this device.

SQUARE POLE SET

The pole is similar to a pool stick. It is about five feet long. We use the pole behind the neck and across our shoulders. Our special teams coach uses the pole with the players when they run down the field to cover kicks so we do not turn the shoulders. We do this drill every day.

Also, we use the pole with our tackles in a pass set drill. We have the pole behind our neck, and we kick back in our pass set. We have then kick and post. We have them reach block with the pole behind their neck and across their shoulders. We have them work the double-team block. If you are trying to teach your linemen to stay square, it is a tremendous device.

When you first have them do this drill, they will have difficulty in keeping the shoulders square. They will tilt the pole one way or the other. They learn to cover their angles and to keep the pole straight. They can feel this with their hands out on the edge of the pole. The art of all of this blocking is a matter of keeping your body in a solid cube, and keeping your feet moving in the cube, without tipping the cube.

We use a drill we call "feet before hands" with the use of the hands. The defender rushes inside, and we move our feet before we use our hands. We call the drills: "Pole, feet before hands."

I do not always subscribe to the theory of how fast you can get your second foot down. The first step is usually some type of power step that has to be set, especially in a man blocking situation. When I am blocking a man, I want to take a deliberate settle read step. From there, I hit on two, or the second step. If I just go step one, step two, and the defender moves, then I have whiffed. You do not have time to adjust to steps three and four.

The use of the term to "get your second foot down as quickly as you can" is used for combination blocks. If I am blocking man, and I take that second step as quickly as I can, and the defender goes inside, I will not be able to even touch the defender if I get that second foot down too quick.

RAIN NOTEPAD

Ray Oliver, our strength coach, found this notepad that you can write on in rainy weather. The military invented this pad. Write this down: www.riteintherain.com.

You get a special pen, and it allows you to write in the rain on the pad. If you are playing or practicing on a rainy day, you can have the info on the notepad that you want for the game or practice that day. It is a neat device that I thought you would be interested in.

WALK-THROUGH BAGS

If a player has a big dummy bag, he is a defensive lineman. If a player has a small dummy bag, he is a linebacker. If the man has no bag, he is a defensive back. If we are working against our defense, we do it that way in our walk-through.

INSIDE MOVES

Never punch on an inside move. If you punch on an inside move, the defender will knock the hand down, and go around you. This is what I do on an inside move. When I set to cover the man, the first move I make is to drop my inside hand. Then I go feet before hands.

There are two ways to make the block. When the defender makes his move, I want to drop my inside hand, move my feet, and then make contact on his outside shoulder and lift. Then, I twist him like a spinning toy top.

If you set nose-to-nose with a guard who goes inside, you must move your feet before you move your hands. Everybody wants to punch the man right away. They get nervous. If you punch before you move your feet, the defender gets your hand and knocks it down and goes around you.

When a defender goes inside, drop your inside hand. This is how we drill it. First, we move the feet and do not use our hands at all.

THE LIFT

Where did I learn the lift? I learned it from Richmond Webb, a player I coached almost 20 years ago. He came to us at the Bengals at the end of his career. If a defender rushed inside against Richmond, he would take his hand and go *whap*. He put his hands on the man, and it was like super glue was on his hands. Later, we had John Jackson, and he did the same thing. When a defender went inside on him, he would club with the inside hand. From that point on, I started teaching tackles that was the way to play it when a defender goes inside. Then, it became the guards' technique on an inside move.

Think about this: It is the same on a Rip move. When a player rips, his feet have to come together. When his feet comes together, you twist him like a toy top, and you stop his momentum by using angular momentum, rather than regular straight lineal momentum to stop him. This prevents the inside knock down of the hand by the defender.

We go from a club to a lift. You can do whatever you want to do with the defender.

PAWING AND JUNCTION READS

Here is a new technique for you. It is pawing, like a Bengal tiger pawing at another animal. It is not a harsh, hard blow, but a soft pawing motion. If we set on a defender, and the defender hesitates, back up and just paw the defender. Keep the hand on him, and by pawing the defender, he will go through the twist we use. If we set on him, and we turn or tilt our inside shoulder, he will come off the block and go inside. If I can stick my hand out before the switch, I will be ready if he comes inside.

I take all of the moves I have covered and call them "junction point" reads and reactions. It is what and how we block a defender. If I cover the defender's body and have the right reaction to his move, then all of the moves will hold up.

A couple of little things I want to cover include the toss crack pulls. Here is an important point for the frontside tackle and guard pulling on the toss crack play. They must get their inside foot deep. It is almost like the first step on a pass block with the inside foot. It is a deep step with the inside foot, and then I make the move outside. A lot of the players want to open too far where they almost turn their back to the line of scrimmage. Some players pull too fast and get knocked off before they can get outside. It is a kick step with the onside foot, and a deep step with the back foot, and then he pulls to the outside.

Now, we look at the tackle-guard pulling on the play. Whenever you have two pullers, you zone block. You may have both the tackle and guard on one man.

SKIP-PULL VS. A MOVING DOUBLE-TEAM

Jim Bowman of Ohio State was the first person I heard talk about the skip-pull. I thought he was nuts when I first saw it. I teach it two ways. I teach it the old way, but I am leaning to the skip-pull more and more. Setting up a drill with the guard and tackle pulling around a stationary dummy on the ground is not a good way to teach the pulling. We want to pull around the double-team block nice and tight. We use the term tight enough so you can strike a match off the butt of the outside man on the double-team.

The thing we get that is different in a game is this: In a game, the double-team block moves inside more. The hole for the puller is not as wide as it was with the dummy on the ground. The hole has moved inside in a game. So we want to be able to skip-pull so we can make that turn up in the hole just off the rear end of the double-team. So you have to adjust the course to tighten down the area where you want the pulling tackle and guard to turn up in. We teach them to skip-pull where they can strike a match off the rear of the double-team block.

ABOUT THE AUTHOR

Paul Alexander is in his 18th season on the Bengals coaching staff, fourth-most in Bengals history. The only Bengals coaches with more seasons are current running back coach Jim Anderson (28), former strength and conditioning coach Kim Wood (28), and former head coach and assistant Dick LeBeau (19).

Alexander is in his 17th straight season as offensive line coach, and he is also the team's assistant head coach, promoted to that position in 2003 when Marvin Lewis took over as head coach.

Alexander's line led a pass protection effort in 2010 that saw the Bengals finish second in the AFC and sixth in the NFL in fewest sacks allowed per passing play. Opponents totaled only 28 sacks in 618 passing plays, an average of one every 22.07 plays.

The Bengals did not allow a sack for 100 consecutive passing plays to close the season. The streak of 100 began in the fourth quarter of game 13 and continued through the final three games. Also in the last three games of the season, the line helped the offense average 34:18 in possession time while posting a 47.8 conversion rate on third downs.

In 2009, the line strongly supported a 10-6 Bengals run to the AFC North Division title. Cincinnati's run blocking helped spring eight rushing games of 100 or more yards by individual backs, breaking the franchise record of six. Three different rushers combined for those eight 100-yarders, only the second time in club history that three rushers had a 100-yard game in a season.

Twice with Alexander's lines, the Bengals have set new franchise records for fewest sacks allowed, led by a record 17 in 2007. In 2005, the total was only 21 sacks allowed. In 2007, as was the case in 2010, the offense allowed no sacks over the final three games. The 2007 total for consecutive passing plays without a sack allowed, to close the season, was 89.

On October 22, 2000, Alexander's line shared the glory of a 278-yard rushing game by running back Corey Dillon versus Denver. It was an NFL record at the time, and it stood fourth in league annals, entering the 2011 season. The Bengals' 407 total rushing yards in that game rank as the fifth-highest single-game total in NFL history, and as the most rushing yards in 60 years. The last team to top it was the New York Giants, who gained 423 against Baltimore in 1950.

Alexander began his NFL coaching career in 1992 as tight ends coach of the New York Jets, under head coach Bruce Coslet. When Coslet moved to Cincinnati as offensive coordinator in 1994, Alexander joined him, in the role of Bengals tight ends coach.

But Alexander's first love in football was always the offensive line. He was afforded the chance to take over that job for the Bengals in 1995, and has held it ever since.

Alexander is a product of distinguished teachers. He coached under Joe Paterno at Penn State and Bo Schembechler at the University of Michigan. He also was offensive line coach at Central Michigan University, a school whose coach, Herb Deromedi, ranks with Paterno and Schembechler among the winningest coaches in NCAA Division I history.

Alexander's birth date is February 12, 1960. He is a native of Rochester, New York, where he attended Cardinal Mooney High School. He was an Academic All-American at SUNY Cortland (NY) and holds a master's degree in exercise physiology from Penn State. Off the field, he is actively involved with the Boy Scouts, the D.A.R.E. program, and high school linemen camps.

He and his wife, Kathy, have three daughters, Mary Beth, Carolyn, and Emily.

ALEXANDER AT A GLANCE

- 2003–present: Cincinnati Bengals, Assistant Head Coach/Offensive Line Coach
- 1994–2002: Cincinnati Bengals, Assistant Coach
- 1992–1993: New York Jets, Assistant Coach
- 1987–1991: Central Michigan University, Assistant Coach
- 1985–1986: University of Michigan, Graduate Assistant
- 1982–1984: Penn State, Graduate Assistant
- 1979–1981: SUNY Cortland, Offensive Tackle

Mike Bloomgren

THE POWER PLAY AND HOW WE TEACH DOUBLE-TEAMS

Stanford University

The first thing I have to tell you is how humbled I am to be here. I have been coming to the C.O.O.L. Clinic ever since I started coaching the offensive line position. I am thrilled to be here and to represent the Stanford program and our head coach, David Shaw. We have a great staff, and we work well together toward a common goal. Luckily for me, they all like the run game and understand the importance of it.

I am going to talk about the power play today. I am going to talk about our double-team block and how we teach the individual blocks.

The first time I heard about the idea of how we now teach the double-team blocks was from Larry Zierlein at this clinic in 2009. When I walked out of here, I was so impressed by how he was moving people. I absolutely loved what I had heard, but I absolutely knew I did not know how to teach it and incorporate it into my world. It was so different from what I was taught as a player and so different than what I was teaching. I went back to Coach Callahan in New York and told him how great it was. We sat on it for a year. Jim McNally came to us as a consultant the next year, and we talked about it and formulated the concepts of what I know now and teach.

The first thing we do when we have our offensive meeting to start the year is to start with a quote from 2010 Hall of Fame inductee Russ Grimm from his induction speech.

There is no greater feeling than to be able to move a man from point A to point B... against his will.

—Russ Grimm

This is what we believe, and we believe it very firmly at Stanford. It is something our kids have bought in to. There is nothing in our offense about leaning on people or position blocking. It just does not come up.

The gap scheme was over a quarter of our total offense in 2011. We ran the gap scheme 261 plays during the year. We averaged 5.67 yards per carry and had a 60.98 percent efficiency. Would I like our efficiency to be up above 80 percent? Absolutely, but this is who we were last year in the fourth quarter. When we were up late in the game, we were running these plays against 10- and 11-man boxes. We were going to go ahead and run these plays to get our three or four yards. An efficient play for us on first and second down is four yards.

When I came to Stanford, they had just come off an Orange Bowl win, where they beat the life out of Virginia Tech. They were already good at running the ball. All I did was come in there and tell them we were going to change how they double-team block and everything about how they block on their base play. You can imagine that I got more than a few people looking at me sideways. It really was not until the fourth game of the year before we were all completely together on the same page.

The University of Washington came down to play us, and they were ranked 15th in the nation. It was a big game with a lot of hype. We went out and ran the gap scheme as well as I have ever been associated with it and set a school record of 446 yards rushing. I cannot tell you how fun it was to be on the field and be a part of it. I was so proud of our guys.

Another reason I like the gap scheme is because of all the other accomplishments it allows us to reach. Yes, we had a pretty good quarterback to help us do a lot of these things. We led the nation in the least number of tackles for a loss, and we led it by a significant margin. A big reason is our gap scheme hits downhill so fast that you just do not have the negative plays, and you are able to stay on track. This is why I am such a big believer in the gap scheme.

When we talk about our double-team technique, we talk about the post and the drive.

POST—INSIDE GUY ON DOUBLE-TEAM

- Jab—gaining ground in your gap. The second step is toward the crotch.
- Flipper/fishhook: Be ready to accept the defensive lineman and go to two hands.
- Block the defender with your body and your gap with your eyes.

If I am talking about the right guard, I am going to take a quick and short four-inch jab step, up and in with my left foot (Diagram #1). The second step is north to the crotch of the defender and slightly ahead of our left foot. It is not a sloop/loop step; it is a very vertical step.

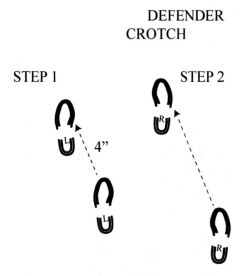

Diagram #1. Post Steps—Right Guard

We are going to put in a single-under fishhook or a flipper, if you want to use the whole surface. We want our pads to come under the defenders' pads. We want pads under pads.

We want to be ready to accept the down lineman and go to two hands if he is fed across our face by the drive blocker. We will talk a little more about that in a minute.

When we drill it in practice, we start on air with five guys across the line. After the jab and crotch steps, we want to advance our stagger down the field for three or four yards. We want to see how quick we can get the second step into the ground.

The next step on post blocking we want to talk about is blocking the defender with our body and our gap with our eyes. We are looking for anything coming through our gap window. If we see somebody passing through our window, we are going to close our window. It does not matter if it is a second-level player like a linebacker coming on a blitz or a down lineman on a stunt.

Here, the left guard is the post man. He takes his jab step with his right foot, and crotch step with his left foot. The center is the drive blocker. The left guard is keeping an eye on his window, the gap between the left guard and left tackle. Once they have movement and he sees the linebacker come to his window, he gets off the double-team and closes his window (Diagram #2). Again, it does not matter if it is a linebacker or another down lineman on a stunt into his window.

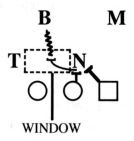

Diagram #2. Closing the Window

DRIVE

- Block the outside man on the double-team.
- Use the high knee technique in the square.
- Get pad under pad.
- Feed the defensive lineman (possible cross shove).
- Stay square to the assigned linebacker.

If I am talking about the right tackle, I am going to have my weight on the right foot and push off it (Diagram #3). I am taking a step to the double-team with my left foot. I am going to close the distance with my right foot and then repeat.

It is very important to get pad under pad. It is amazing how much power you have when you get your pad under the opponents' pad. He stays low and square as he is advancing his stagger. He must stay low so that he comes up and through, like a jack-in-the-box, under the pad of the defender as he is knocking or feeding him across to the post player.

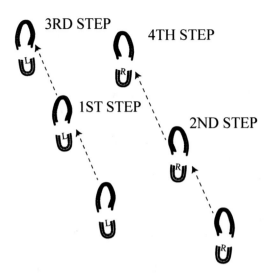

Diagram #3. Drive Steps—Right Tackle

He must stay square to his assigned linebacker. Once he turns his shoulders, there is nothing he can do to stop the linebacker from running over the top. We have all seen it happen, and we have to coach against it.

DOUBLE-TEAM MUSTS

- Get movement on the line of scrimmage.
- Stay square to the second level.
- Close the window.
- Get removal.

This is not anything that you have not heard before. We preach this and preach this over and over.

We want to take care of the line of scrimmage and get movement to get this thing started. You have to handle the second level. You have to go two-for-two. Linebackers are too good to not block them, but we have to get movement on the line of scrimmage first. We do not have to be in a hurry because the deuce or the trey is going to the Will linebacker. You have plenty of time. Of course, we are going to close the window with the post player if we need to. We want to get removal on whoever we touch. We stay on the double-team as long as we can, until the drive man takes on his responsibility at the second level. We are in no hurry to move to a linebacker running laterally.

In practice, it looks like this (Diagram #4). The drive player doubles with the right guard. The drive

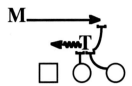

Diagram #4. Deuce Power Right

player drives the defensive tackle from on outside shade to an inside shade, and the guard takes him from there. The drive player then picks up the linebacker as he flows to the play. He must stay square.

We would love for the tackle to build the wall and seal the linebacker in if they are flowing like "big dogs," but that is not always reality. We tell the tackle to "U" him out. All that means is to get on him and take him where he wants to go. Take the defender past the hole, and let the running back run straight downhill.

If the 3 technique defensive tackle spikes out, we block it like this (Diagram #5). The post player will jab and crotch block. He accelerates his feet, goes to two hands, and washes the defensive tackle as flat as he can. The post player is already square, and he transitions to the second level.

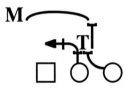

Diagram #5. 3 Technique Spike

If we have a run-through by the linebacker into the guard's window, we make this adjustment (Diagram #6). We tell the drive blocker if he sees something flash inside and feels the guard leave, he has to transition to two hands right now and wash the defender flat down the line of scrimmage.

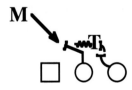

Diagram #6. Run-Through

I often get asked about our splits because of the post and drive high leg. We legitimately do not worry about it. Our normal split is a two-foot split.

One adjustment we make with a head-up defensive tackle on our guard is we immediately go to two hands. We still have the same footwork, but we do not have an outside fishhook or outside flipper; we go to two hands right away. Nothing changes for the drive and the high leg man.

Another question I get all of the time is how can we post and drive if we do not have the big offensive linemen you have at the college and pro levels? We have taught it to a 220-pound wide receiver we had to put in at tight end. It was day 13 in spring practice, and the only position he had ever played was wide receiver. He was the drive man. It was not textbook, but after teaching him the concept, he was able to drive the defensive tackle enough to push him into our guard, and he was able to get in the way of the linebacker enough at the second level to give the back a chance. He was a wide receiver who was a willing blocker. That is all we need.

We teach the choke block, the back block, and the down block all the same. You may want to choke back on a backside shade, a back block on a 3 technique, or a down block on the frontside.

CHOKE, BACK, OR DOWN BLOCK

- Drive your knee toward the defender.
- Hit in the V of the neck of the defender.
- Use a split hand punch.
- Get removal.

We have all seen it where you tell somebody to take a positive step when you are blocking down on somebody. They lift their directional foot up, and it ends up behind them. We have found that if we tell them to drive their knee toward the target, their foot cannot help but to follow. We want to hit in the V of the defender's neck, between their shoulder and their ear. We use a split hand punch, meaning one on the side and one upfield. The second step is so important to get it into the ground immediately. We want to put our back foot where the defender's back foot just left from, and just keep driving.

PULLING GUARD

- Think about where you will find your linebacker.
- Skip pull.
- Come tight around the double-team. Strike a match.
- Be alert to swab color in the C gap on your way to your linebacker.
- Be square when you attack the linebacker.
- Wing set should be one hole wider.

It is important for the pulling guard to not only know who they are going to block, but also where he will be. When they are in their stance, they should be thinking where they will find their linebacker. Obviously, it has a lot to do with where the double-team is.

A lot of people do not like to skip pull. We have our players skip pull and it keeps our players square (Diagram #7). If we have our left guard skip pull, he is going to take his outside foot on the snap and bring it behind his up field or post foot, and then let it open him up as he is going to attack.

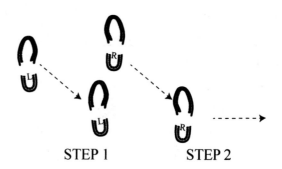

Diagram #7. Left Guard Skip Pull

We want them to come tight around the double-team. The visual we give them is we want them to be able to strike a match off the double-team with our inside hip.

We want them to be alert to swab color in the C gap. That means if someone is losing on a block at the point of attack, we want him to hit the defender with his outside shoulder and deliver him back to the person responsible for blocking him, as he squares up for the linebacker. It might be the fullback with C gap responsibility. It could be the tight end blocking a 6 technique. If we are flat out getting beat in the C gap, he is going to blow color up. In a perfect world, we will swab color, but if we are getting beat, we are going to take him on so we get the play started. Remember that is what we are all about. Get the play started with no negatives.

Obviously, we want the guard to be square when he attacks the linebacker. We want to attack, inside-out on the pull. We tell them to kick the linebacker out until we can't see him in the hole. If the linebacker is running at all, we should be able to pry him out of the hole.

TWO-STEP HINGE

- Execute true two steps down.
- Block anything B gap until the center makes contact.
- Hinge back; throw your shoulder into the next defender outside.

Another block we need to talk about is the two-step hinge on the backside (Diagram #8). This is what we want the backside to do. The two steps down is a shuffle, shuffle. He will block anything that shows in the B gap until the center makes contact and then throw his shoulder into the next outside defender. We want to throw the shoulder violently. If he has to stay down to cover the B gap for too long before he can hinge, we want him to at least get his arm out there to shove or force the backside defender upfield. We have tackles today with great length. We want to use that length to our advantage. Make the defender run around it. The difference between knocking him off track could be the difference between a one-yard loss and getting the play started. If we get the play started, we know good things can happen.

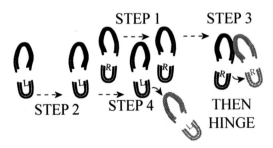

Diagram #8. Two-Step Hinge

Here is our power left play (Diagram #9). We will look at it from both sides of the line.

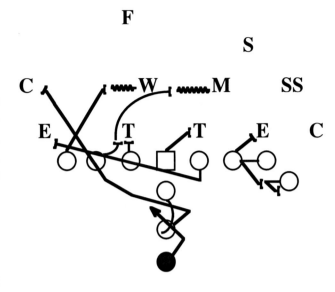

Diagram #9. Power Left

Power right may look something like this with a different front and formation (Diagram #10). Notice the left tackle helps the center and then protects the backside.

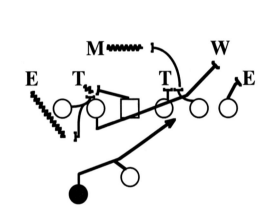

Diagram #10. Power Right

I want to spend some time on big people runs and run-action passes. With run-action passes, the emphasis is on the run and calling out. This is how we draw up a play with our giant formation (Diagram #11). We take our left tackle and put him at right tight end. We put our sixth offensive lineman in at the left tackle and our seventh lineman in as the fourth lineman on the right.

The objective is to get good looks. It is the old option principle about not running to bad looks.

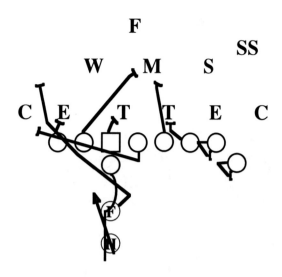

Diagram #11. Giant Right, Power Left

We want to know where we have the number advantage. We can run giant right, power right if the numbers are better for us (Diagram #12).

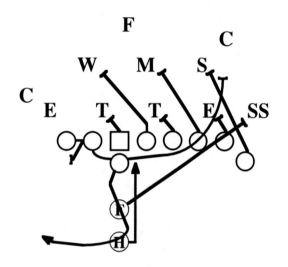

Diagram #12. Giant Right, Power Right

I really like the numbers and angles in this situation. You should not have a defensive hat show up too early in this situation.

This is a diagram we used in our bowl game against Oklahoma State University (Diagram #13). It is just a way for us to come with the wing to the two-man side and have a power king type of concept. We want to work the wing and the tackle to bury the defensive end and then get up to the Will linebacker.

The first time we ran it was against the University of Arizona, and they played a Bear front defense and

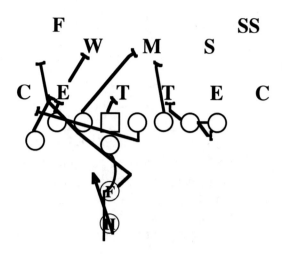

Diagram #13. Monster Right, Power Left

brought the two safeties to our strongside. We ran the weakside stutter play, as they call it in the NFL. We got a kick by the right guard and a wrap by the fullback, and the runner was rolling. Why do we end up with some of these plays looking so easy? It is my belief that so many defensive coordinators are worried about what you are doing on the frontside, in terms of making a C, D, E, and F gap at times, and worried about fits that they outthink themselves. In fact, one of the things I have seen during games is a defensive coordinator lining up his players in a walk-through on the sideline between series. That is when I knew we needed to run more of that stuff. It does create problems for the defense.

The other thing I like about having seven linemen on the field is that you are preparing guys to play. When we played USC, we had one of our defensive tackles gets his ankle rolled up, and he goes down for a couple of series. The kid that stepped in did a great job for us. He had already played 15 snaps that game in our big people sets. The game was not brand new to him. I think that has tremendous value for us.

Let me finally get to the run-action pass. This can be some exciting stuff. We had already run 10 to 12 snaps of big people running plays against Arizona. They were playing us in a Bear front type of goal line defense. Our offensive coordinator calls up a counter pass (Diagram #14).

As it turned out, the only person close enough to cover our tight end was our other tight end. If you are going to live in that world, the run-action passes have tremendous value. They get safeties out of the play better than anything else we can do. It is

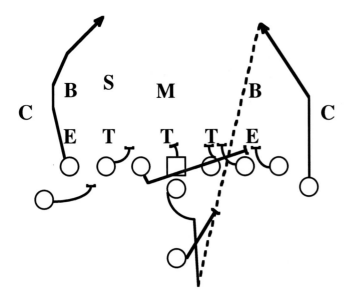

Diagram #14. Counter Pass

better than trying to have receivers dig them out. If you can run one of these plays in your opening 10 to 15 plays, I think it will do a lot for you.

ABOUT THE AUTHOR

Mike Bloomgren joined the Stanford staff as offensive line coach on February 23, 2011, after spending four seasons with the New York Jets, where he served as assistant offensive coordinator (2010), offensive assistant (2009), and offensive quality control coach (2007–2008).

His work with the Cardinals' offensive line, which included three first-year starters last season, played a pivotal role in providing protection for quarterback Andrew Luck to complete over 70 percent of his passes and throwing a school-record 37 touchdowns, in addition to compiling the third-highest rushing total in school annals.

Right guard David DeCastro was a unanimous All-America selection and finalist for the Outland Trophy, while left tackle Jonathan Martin earned first team Walter Camp Football Foundation and American Football Coaches Association All-America honors. Redshirt freshmen David Yankey and Cameron Fleming were all-conference honorable mention selections in their first seasons of collegiate competition.

As run game coordinator, Bloomgren's play calling and schemes aided Stanford in compiling the third-highest single-season rushing output in school history with 2,738 yards.

Prior to joining the Jets, Bloomgren served as offensive coordinator at Delta State University for the 2005 and 2006 seasons, where the Statesmen passed for over 7,500 yards in two seasons and advanced to the semifinals of the NCAA Division II playoffs in 2006.

He also worked as a co-offensive coordinator at Catawba College from 2002 to 2004, where he helped the Indians to the South Atlantic Conference title in 2003 and NCAA Division II playoff appearances in 2002 and 2004.

Bloomgren worked under both Mike Dubose and Dennis Franchione as a graduate assistant at Alabama from 1999–2001, helping the Tide to the 1999 Southeastern Conference championship. He launched his coaching career as an undergraduate assistant for Bobby Bowden at Florida State University, where the Seminoles captured a pair of ACC titles (1997–1998) during his tenure.

A 1999 graduate of Florida State with a bachelor's degree in sports management, Bloomgren earned his master's degree in higher education from the University of Alabama in 2001.

A native of Tallahassee, Florida, Mike and his wife, Lara have two sons, Tyler and Parker.

BLOOMGREN AT A GLANCE

- 1991–2001: Alabama, Graduate Assistant
- 2002–2004: Catawba College, Co-Offensive Coordinator
- 2005–2006: Delta State, Offensive Coordinator
- 2007–2009: New York Jets, Offensive Quality Control
- 2009: New York Jets, Offensive Assistant
- 2010: New York Jets, Assistant Offensive Coordinator

Dan Dorazio

DOUBLE-UNDER AND SINGLE-UNDER BLOW DELIVERY AND RUN BLOCKING TECHNIQUES

British Columbia Lions

I am privileged and honored to have this opportunity. We are humbled to share our thoughts tonight. There is nothing I know that I have not learned from someone else. We have greatly admired and respected the many clinicians that have been organized at the C.O.O.L Clinic in the past. We have learned from some of the giants in our industry. People like Howard Mudd, Jim McNally, Jim Hanifan, Joe Bugle, and John Matsko, who have been so instrumental in some of our strong thoughts and ideas about football.

We have also learned the hard way. We have suffered some incredibly painful lessons by getting our butts kicked on game day. There is no question that we cannot be in a competitive football game today without a highly skilled football team. You cannot have a highly skilled football team unless you have good players. You cannot have good players unless you have excellent techniques and fundamentals. You cannot have excellent techniques and fundamentals unless you practice those things, very well. The fun in fundamentals comes from winning on game day. It is a bunch of tough hard work done day in and day out. It never changes; it is a lot of hard work.

Mike Maser, an outstanding offensive line coach, said in this very room a few years back: "The mother of all learning is repetition." Mike went on to say that day that repetition has got to be an accepted way of life for offensive linemen.

A note to the head coaches and offensive coordinators in the audience: do not overoffense your offensive line coach. Do less, better. The game plan is way overrated. Execution is far too underrated these days.

Following are three things that have a major effect on the outcome of most blocks:

- Creation of leverage
- Alignment of five body parts on the cylinder of the defender, and the role they play
- Creation of force

The creation of leverage is created by striking the cylinder of the defender, low enough with the hands, the forearms, or the shoulders at a point low enough on that cylinder to lift the cylinder up and at the very same time, close enough to segment the upper body strength of the defender from the power in his hips and legs. Close enough that the center of gravity of the blocker is as close as possible to the center of gravity of the defender. At that point, he is hitting it close enough.

THE FIVE BODY PARTS

- The first body part is a combination of the eyes and the head. Where the eyes go, the head goes. Where the head goes, the body goes. Its function is to provide direction for the block.
- The second body part is a combination of the hands, the forearms, and the shoulders. They constitute the blocking surface. These are the strike force of the blocker.
- The third body part is the back. The back functions in two ways. First, it serves as a ram rod. Second, it serves as a balancer. When the back arches after initial contact, it allows the blocker's balance to get back over his feet.
- The fourth major body part is a combination of the hips, the butt, the legs, and the knees. The muscles in the butt and in the legs are the largest, most powerful muscles the good Lord gave us. With the knees pointing in all of the time, that part of the body functions as the delivery system. They are going to deliver the power into the block.

- The final body portion is the feet. The feet function two ways. Number one, they provide a platform for the blocker. Number two, they create movement for the blocker.

The *Webster's Dictionary* defines force this way: "driving or propelling against resistance." Resistance in football is the playing surface. When the feet move sooner, quicker, or wider against the surface, energy is created, and movement occurs. When all five body parts are on a 45-degree angle through the cylinder of the defender, you have a fighting chance to knock somebody's butt back off the ball.

In the remaining time we have here, let us talk about the double-under and single-under blow delivery and the roles they have within the techniques we use.

As we move into double-under blow delivery, the first drill to show you on film is the low hands drill. I have to credit John Strollo from Penn State. We have learned so much from him on this blow delivery. We start out in a squat position with our hands out front and below our knees. The players have a little three-inch ball they roll between their fingers as they move forward for five yards, keeping the same position. The objective is to carry the hands below the knees, move your feet a little bit, and feel your elbows in tight close to your ribs.

Next, we move to the six-point double-under. We put the offensive player in a six-point stance, on their knees, but not on their hands. There is a person positioned just over them with a 13-pound medicine ball at the offensive player's shoulder level. The offensive player strikes an upward blow on the bottom of the medicine ball with his hands. The objectives are two things. We are going to isolate the eyes, and we are going to isolate the hands. The blow delivery is open palms, thumbs are open and at a 45-degree angle so the elbows stay tight to the body. We want to strike crisply and lift slightly. The eyes are locked, big, and intense. We have our guys clap just prior to delivering the blow. We call this coupling. We want coupled hands when we strike the surface of the cylinder. Only then do the hands come apart.

The next phase is a two-point double-under from a two-point stance. Hands start below the knees. We are going to add one body part here. At this point, when the hands strike the ball, we tell them we want a butt squeeze. The hands trigger the butt squeeze.

We move on to hands bring feet double-under. Now, when the hands strike, they trigger the butt squeeze, and then we bring our feet for two steps. The hands strike before the feet move. It is always hands first, feet second. The objective is hands bring the feet. From there, we bring our feet. The same techniques as before, bringing our hands from low to high, but we bring and chop our feet for five or six steps.

Let us take it one step further, this time without the medicine ball. We will now add the back. We start our chin to the chest of the defender. The offensive lineman is squatting slightly below the defender, both in a two-point stance. The offensive lineman has his hands locked behind his back. What is our objective here? Number one, we want to separate our hat on contact. This is very important. Number two, we want to arch our back on contact. Number three, you go press your hips on his hips. Finally, number four, move and chop your feet to step on his toes with your toes for a few yards. Once you have separated your hat, arched your back, and put your hips to his hips, your center of gravity is next to the center of gravity of the defender. Arching the back allows the blocker to get his center of gravity over his feet. Finishing means getting your weight back over your feet. That is the bottom line objective we are trying to get out of this.

Let us talk about the leverage that we talked about before. We said we wanted to hit a defender low enough to create lift. We start out this next drill with the blocker in a two-point stance. The defender is in the same position he was in with the medicine ball, but instead of the ball, he now has his hands folded at eye level to the offensive lineman. The offensive player has his palms up and on the underside of the defender's crossed arms, at the point of impact on the cylinder of the defender. He hits the defender and lifts him. We are using the same techniques that lead us to this point. His hips are pressed up to the hips of the defender, and he brings and chops his feet. This unweights the defender, who is lifted up on his toes as he is backpedaling. If you want a guy to get the feel of leverage, do this drill. Believe me, he will feel it. We want to lift, squeeze your butt, arch your back, separate your hat, press your hips to his hips, and step on his toes as you lift up. You unweight the defender.

Finally, we want to put it all together. We said this. There are five body parts that were important to the impact of the block. The five are the head, the forearms (or hands or shoulders), the back, the hips and legs, and the feet. We said if they are all in line through the cylinder of the defender on a 45-degree angle line of force, with my body parts on his body parts, I am going to have a pretty good line of force. I am going to be able to create pretty good leverage. Watch the hat separate, the elbows in tight, lift, the back arch, the butt squeeze, and now come bring your feet. Get your center of gravity on his center of gravity. We are adding the last body part here. Move your feet sooner, move them quicker, and move them wider.

When we talk about force, we are talking about driving and propelling your feet against resistance. Resistance in football is the playing surface. We always want the knees in; we really do not care where the toes are. Some linemen like their toes pointed out when they are driving a defender. Get the feet to move sooner and quicker. Your feet cannot ever be wide enough in run blocking.

A variation on the two-point double-under drill we like is with a brace step. You start in the same position, but this time you take a short brace step with one foot, and then make contact with the medicine ball. The key is to dip the opposite knee in order to lower your center of gravity. The brace step lowers the opposite knee to lower the hips. When the hands drop, we clap to get coupled, and then we lift up and bring our feet. Everything is put together. The most important thing is the center of gravity is lowered. Let's take a look at the game film to see these techniques in use. (Film)

We also use the single-under technique. We begin to train this with the hand on the ground in a three-point stance and bring it up to the cylinder of the defender with our elbow tight. The hand comes first, and then the knee and the feet follow. We want to get the foot down and come over the knee.

The next step is from a two-point stance, and we do the same thing. Sometimes, we line the defender on the outside shoulder. The offensive player has to shuffle a little bit to widen. Then, they shoot a single-under with their inside hand to the cylinder of the defender. We want to see the elbow in tight and a lift up. The single-under is the same as a double-under. The elbow is in tight, and you lift up. Run blocking is lifting and not so much pushing. There are no windups in what we do.

We also practice a double-team single-under. Again, we put the defender on the outside shoulder of the blocker. We shuffle over to get in position, and then we shoot a single-under with the outside hand and lift up. Hit and then bring the feet, suck the butt, put your hips on his hips, and move the feet.

We teach a wrench technique with the single- or double-under. At the point of attack, when the blocker is fitted square on the defender and the back makes a cut, the defender will try to come off. The blocker can feel him trying to come off. At that point, we want to wrench the inside elbow. Hold the elbow inside and in tight as you keep a high knee. The elbow wrenches inward when he feels the blocker trying to come off. (Film)

I want give you something that I learned from Larry Bechtel 34 years ago. I have been carrying this around for 34 years. It is a fumble recovery drill. It is really an agility fumble recovery drill (Diagram #1). We are coaching ball security and cradling the body around the ball.

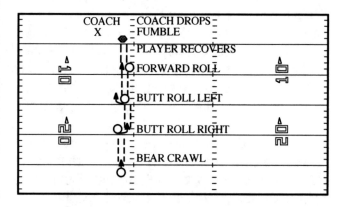

Diagram #1. Fumble Recovery Drill

Another thing we do is a grip drill, even during the season. We do it every day during the off-season. We have a tub of sand that is about 15" x 24" x 12" deep. Our linemen throw their hands into the sand, alternating one after the other, and constrict their fingertips into the sand. Basically, they are squeezing the sand and clinching their fists. It strengthens the hands. Everything we do in football is done with the hands.

Another drill to strengthen the hands is to alternately drop and catch two 10-pound weights that are taped together to form one, in between our legs, from a sitting position. This helps with grip strength.

The last drill I will show you for hand strength is good. We have our guys pick up a 125-pound dumbbell in each hand. We want them to hold it for 90 seconds in a standing position. See if your guys can do it. It is darn tough. My guys can barely hold it for 90 seconds.

Thank you very much.

ABOUT THE AUTHOR

Dan Dorazio enters his 40th year of coaching, his 15th CFL campaign and 10th with the Lions as offensive line coach.

In 2011, the Lions surrendered a league-low 29 sacks marking the first time since 1995 that the club registered the fewest sacks against. Anchored by All-Canadian center Angus Reid and West Division Most Outstanding Lineman Jovan Olafioye, Dorazio's squad led the way as the offense racked up 6,646 total yards in 2011.

Dorazio's professional coaching career began in Calgary in 1998 as the Stamps' offensive line coach. He enjoyed five successful seasons in Calgary (1998–2002) and earned two Grey Cup championships (1998, 2001).

Dorazio's lengthy coaching career began in 1972 as a student assistant at Kent State University. He would eventually earn the role of coaching the team's tight ends in 1974 before moving to the University of Hawaii in 1975, where he remained until 1977. The following season, he joined the staff at San Jose State University for one year before continuing his coaching career at the University of Washington in 1979.

Dorazio would eventually make stops in the University of Northern Iowa (1980–1981), Georgia Tech (1982–1983), the University of Washington (1984–1988), College of the Holy Cross (1989–1991), and the University of Maryland (1992–1996). Dan's final season in the college ranks before moving to the CFL was at Boston University in 1997.

Dorazio hails from Pittsburgh, Pennsylvania, and graduated from Kent State in 1974 with a bachelor's degree in education. Dorazio and his wife, Lisa, live in Abbotsford, British Columbia. He has two children, Daniel and Marisa.

Pat Flaherty

COMBINATION RUN AND PASS PROTECTION TECHNIQUES

New York Giants

Thank you, Bob. Coaches, top of the morning to you. My hat is off to the coaches who went from here after last night's session to the upstairs and continued with the clinic. The thing about offensive line coaches is they know how to grind. They will spend hours talking to one another about football or talking about line play in general. That is something that is very special. That is one reason I came back to speak at Bob's clinic. Before that, it was Jim McNally's clinic. I have sat in your seats many times and listened to coaches give their presentations.

When I give my presentation today, you will see some things that will look familiar to you. You will say, "I heard Tony Wise say those same things before." You will be right. I am going to plagiarize some of his material and that of many other coaches. I use it because it works. That is the bottom line. If it works, use it.

This clinic is one of the best sources of information I know. I say that because many outstanding coaches have come to this clinic to lecture. During my vacation, if I do not have the opportunity to attend this clinic, I watch the DVDs of the speakers from this clinic. I have done that for a number of years. Each time I do that, I pick up at least one thing that I install and use. I think that is the great thing about coming to clinics.

We heard some great presentations last night from all the coaches who spoke. The techniques and fundamentals they spoke about is what work for them. What works for the New York Giants is what my presentation will be this morning. That does not mean that what I say is different or it is better than anyone else's schemes. All the coaches are a little different, but the players are a little different in each coach's situation.

The individual players we coach have a different make-up with their physical appearance and their mental approach. We have to coach the players we have with the techniques that work for them. We have to make adjustments because of the length of the torso, height, or flexibility of the individual players. In a perfect world, all the linemen on the offensive line would look alike in their stance. They should all have the same knee bend and body position. However, it does not work that way.

You have to give your players parameters on getting into a stance based on how you feel as their offensive line coach.

We won the Super Bowl in 2007 and again this year in 2012. Having the opportunity to win the Super Bowl in 2007 and to come back and do it again is special. I cannot explain how that feels. I feel very fortunate to have had that chance. Do I feel that I am any better than other coaches because I had that opportunity? That is a simple "No."

In 2004, when I came to the New York Giants, I followed a legend as an offensive line coach. I followed Jim McNally as the offensive line coach of the Giants. Even though he was not in the building any longer, he was very helpful with my transition into that job. He was the sounding board, and I asked him about the players he coached. I thought he did a phenomenal job of coaching those players.

Every year, you change some players and bring in new talent. When you come into a new program, you have to find the best pieces that fit what you want to do. In my opinion, the one player we got who has been phenomenal for us is Eli Manning. As a rookie and into his second year, some people did not know whether he could do the job. However, everyone who went to work with him every day knew he was going to be good because of the way he approached things.

I want to get started, but if you have any questions about anything, throw up your hand and

I will try to answer them. The first thing I want to get into is how to develop offensive linemen.

OFFENSIVE LINEMAN DEVELOPMENT

Mentally—Be the best:
- Play the play longer than my opponent.
- Know your assignment and your teammate's assignments.

Physically—Take your drill work to your team work:
- Perfect your technique, footwork, and hat and hand placement.
- Execute your block with power, balance, and relentless effort.

An offensive lineman's mentality has to be the desire to be the best offensive lineman. That is what you want from a player. I will quote a number of coaches in this presentation. Mike Sweatman was our special teams coordinator in Chicago and New York. He is now retired. He always said to play the play longer than your opponent does. That statement makes sense. The play is never the same length as far as time is concerned. It could be four, five, six, or seven seconds. It is the same idea as when contact occurs in a block. Does the contact occur on the first, second, third, or fourth steps?

That depends on what technique the defender plays and how far the offensive lineman is off the line of scrimmage. One thing I know is the offensive lineman must have his second step on the ground because contact could come that early.

The statement about knowing your assignment and your teammate's assignment goes back to when you started playing football. Everyone wanted to be the quarterback. However, the coach or your father told you, you were going to be a center, guard, or tackle. The first thing you had to do was learn your assignment. That assignment was to block "him." Whatever rule it was, you learned to block your man. After you learned to block "him," you had to learn the adjacent lineman's assignment. After you mastered that bit of knowledge, you learned what the backs and quarterback were doing.

To develop the offensive lineman physically, he must take his drill work to his team work. He has to perfect his technique. He must learn the proper footwork and learn where to place his helmet and hands. Those things lead to executing the block by using power, balance, and relentless effort. What else can you ask of an offensive lineman? The last thing you can ask is for them to finish what they start.

 ## OFFENSIVE LINEMEN

- The offensive line is the heart of the team.
- Huddle posture is to break the huddle and get to the line of scrimmage.
- Poise: Good or bad, you must put the past play behind you and focus on the next play.
- Example: Exhibit through your play—fast, furious, and physical.

I believe the offensive line is the heart of the team. I think all the coaches in this room believe that also. That is the last thing we say as a group after we finish warm-ups and before we leave the field after practice. Good and bad things are going to happen, but we have to make sure we take ownership in the huddle. The quarterback is the leader, and we all know that. However, the offensive linemen must do some things to settle everyone down.

We want to break the huddle and run to the line of scrimmage. We say run because if we say jog to the line of scrimmage, they will walk. If we say walk, they will crawl. We tell them to run to the line of scrimmage, to get down, and to get set.

The offensive line has to exercise poise. They cannot dwell on the previous play. If it was a bad play, forget about it, and focus on the next play. That is the most important play of the game. We want to work to improve during the game. If we score a touchdown, we come to the bench and talk about what was good and what went wrong. After that, we send them out to score another touchdown. Play the next play, not the last one.

The offensive line has to set the example for the team. The offensive line has to set the tempo of the game. We want them to play fast, furious, and physical. They have to set the tempo for the entire offense.

At the Giants practice facility in our locker room, we do not have many big signs all over the walls. However, we have some signs that relate to the way we play. I know everyone knows Russ Grimm. He is a Hall of Fame offensive guard. He has spoken at this clinic, and Joe Moore coached him. He made this statement, and we have it posted in our room. He said, "There is no greater feeling than to be able to move a man from point A to point B against his will." That is what we are going to talk about today. We are going to talk about moving the defender with vertical leverage in the run and pass games.

TRUST YOUR TECHNIQUE

You must first master each technique, which takes quality full speed work, both mentally and physically. Approach your drill work with pride and determination to be the best. The first question is: "What is your technique?" The technique is what you teach. However, you must perfect the technique before you can trust it.

It is interesting to think about coaching a freshman in high school, a freshman in college, or a rookie in the NFL and teaching him a particular technique that will transform him into being what you want him to be. You teach him the way you want him to look and execute. You want the feet and hands a certain way. You teach him the knee bend and flat back in the stance. However, it may be difficult for him to do the things you want done. He has to do it repeatedly until he becomes good at doing what you want him to do.

If players have enough repetitions doing the techniques the proper and correct way, they will become good at doing them. That is particularly important in pass protection. If the offensive blocker has to block a great pass rusher with a number of pass rushing moves, he has to trust his techniques. If the offensive lineman does not learn to trust his techniques, he will panic. That is what the defense tries to do to the offensive line. They want the offensive linemen to panic.

Most of you coaches in this room have strength and conditioning coaches. I am an offensive line coach and not the strength and conditioning coach. I make that very clear to our players. We are going to teach drills, and we do not want to waste a rep. We teach the drills and do the repetitions with effort.

We want them to do the rep and do it right to the best of their ability. However, if the lineman did not step the correct way, or was not low enough, or did something else wrong, we repeat the rep. We do not repeat the rep to give the defender another rep or because an offensive lineman did not give the effort he needed to give. Drills are for teaching techniques and not for conditioning. We do not waste reps.

OUTWORK YOUR OPPONENT

- *Mental:* Be smarter, and prepare better than your opponent.
- *Physical:* Be stronger, and have pride with your techniques and fundamentals.
- *Verbal:* Be great communicators.

The first statement is to be smart and prepare better than your opponent. How do you know you prepared better than your opponent did? You do not know that. You do not know how the opponent is going to prepare. However, we do not want to leave any stone unturned. Do everything you can possibly do to prepare them. Do not leave anything to chance. That is how we prepare.

LEVERAGE

- *Vertical:* Pad under pad (PUP)
- *Horizontal:* Position pertaining to the hole

We teach vertical leverage, and that is how we want to play the game. We want our pads under their pads. We want our pads lower than the defender. A long time ago, I worked for a coach by the name of Dick Anderson at Penn State University. Through the years with Dick, and various other coaches including Bob Wylie, I learned there are different techniques for doing things. However, the most important thing I learned was about leverage.

If you have two wrestlers with the same size and strength, the one with the best leverage can take the other wrestler down. That is a proven fact in today's wrestling. However, when we taught wrestling back then, it was nothing but playing football on a mat. All we did was transfer that fact to the football field, and that is what we taught in the offensive line.

Defensive coaches teach their players to be responsible for a particular gap. Offensive coaches teach their players to knock the defender out of that gap. In some cases, it may take two offensive linemen to accomplish that feat. The offensive linemen control what we do in the game on offense. We know the snap count and the play, and we can roll off the ball. When the offensive line comes off the ball, the back has a place to run the football.

Horizontal leverage is getting in position as it pertains to the hole. If the offensive blocker can get his helmet to the outside of a defender playing on his outside shoulder, the defensive coach will rip the defender a new one. The defensive coach aligned the defender in that gap so he could maintain gap integrity to the outside. He does not want the offensive blocker to reach the defender. That is fine with the offensive lineman. He does not have to reach the defender; however, he has to get vertical leverage on the defender. He has to drive him off the line of scrimmage at a 45-degree angle. If the offensive lineman can do that, the back can gain yardage inside of him.

You do not need to do that type of blocking all day long. If it is necessary to seal the B gap, block down on the defender from the outside, and pull the guard around the defender. That is what I am going to talk about in the running game. After that, I will talk about some pass protections.

The last thing an offensive lineman must do is finish every play. We have always talked about finishing as part of our techniques, and now the entire football team is talking about it. The offensive line has to take credit for those thoughts, and we should. When an offensive lineman finishes something, everyone will follow the example and do it. They do it because they see what happens when you finish a block.

If the offensive line is having a bad day at the office and the defense is winning, there is a look in the eyes of the quarterback, running back, and receivers. If the offensive line cannot get it done, they start to get nervous. You have to finish every block, and it all starts in the drills. In the drills, as the blocker gets to the end of each block, the coach has to yell, "Finish!" Take it one step further, and explain to them what you mean by the term "finish."

Doug Collins, the Philadelphia 76ers basketball coach, talked about finishing what you start. He said, "If you have faith, you have hope; and if you have hope, you have life." That simply means: it is never over until the fat lady sings.

NO EXCUSES

- There are *reasons* for everything.
- There are *no excuses* for anything.

We have this posted in our room. When we talk to our rookies, we have a dialog we use. If they make a mistake, we ask them what they are doing. The first thing they say "I thought." When he gets a little more experience, the answer to that question is "I saw." That is an improvement in his development. As he develops further, we ask him why he blocked that man instead of a different defender. He says, "I screwed up." The bottom line is "I thought" and "I saw" are reasons, but there are no excuses. You have to establish that thought with your linemen.

RUN BLOCKING PROGRESSION

The first thing you have to do is to define what run blocking progression is.

Line Posture

- *Horizontal alignment:* The split for the guards is two feet from the center. The tackles are two and a half feet from the guard.
- *Vertical alignment:* The linemen align their head on the belt of the center.

These are general rules, which we adjust to different situations. We move six inches in and out, depending on the situation. In short yardage and goal line, we cut the splits down so we can come off the ball more aggressively. We adjust the vertical alignment also. We want to be legal in our alignment at all times. However, we adjust the alignment according to the play or offense we run. We can move up, depending on the defensive alignment or situation. We want to adjust our line posture to attack the defensive front concept.

STANCE

Everyone has a way to teach the stance. At the New York Giants, we teach the stance this way.

- Align in a three-point stance.
- Balanced/explosive and be able to move in four directions.
- Down hand aligns outside of the "near" eye.
- The off arm-elbow is tight to the rib cage.
- Strain your eyes through the eyebrows.

All of our offensive linemen move in four different directions. They must reach block right/left, pull to the right/left, come straight off the ball, and pass protect. The center and tackles pull at times in our offense. Their stance must remain the same balanced and explosive stance regardless of what the play is. We do not want to tip what we are doing by the way we get into a stance.

I used to use the term "comfortable" in regards to the stance. I do not use that word anymore. I do not know if there is a comfortable stance. When I played football in college, I was never comfortable in a football uniform. That was especially true when I had coaches screaming at me, and I had some great coaches who coached me. I was never comfortable in the uniform, but I was always told to get in an explosive stance.

People want to know how to get into an explosive stance. To start, you set your feet, you bend your knees, and put your hand down. Where you put your down hand is up to you. We put it outside the near eye. When we put the hand on the ground, we want five fingernails in the ground. I see linemen all the time in a three-point stance with two fingernails in the ground. He may as well be in a two-point stance.

We can rest the off elbow on the thigh board, but I want it tight to the rib cage. From the stance, when the lineman steps, everything that he has comes forward into the defender. It is like firing a bullet into the defender. He wants to strain and look through his eyebrows. If he lifts his head, his ass goes down. In our stance, we want the butt higher than the shoulders. If he lifts his head to look at the defense, his butt is lower than the shoulders.

DRILL PROGRESSION

In our drill work, we work on what we call "offensive line demeanor." On our practice field, the offensive line practice area is marked with squares (Diagram #1). We place shields on the ground and align by position on a line to work on footwork. Every day, we work on two-step starts. We work on the first two steps in the reach and drill blocks. You put the shields on the ground, and you never move them. That allows you to go fast and get a tremendous amount of repetitions.

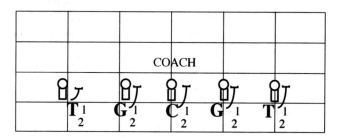

Diagram #1. Two-Step Drill

In the drill, we repeatedly teach, "Chest on the thigh, and eyes on the landmark." Every time we say, "Set, hut," we follow that with, "Chest on the thigh, eyes on the landmark." If they do not do it, we repeat the rep. The offensive lineman is controlling the environment. When he steps, he has to bend to get his chest on his thigh and get the leverage he needs. He has to see the landmark with his eyes. If he does not do that, something is wrong. We do this drill most days because it does not take time to do the drill. It goes quick, and we get valuable reps.

We can expand the drill and include a cutoff block. We give the linemen a direction, and they perform the cutoff block in that direction. If I give them a right direction, the right guard and tackle do not have a cutoff block. Instead of a cutoff block, they perform a square pull or trap pull technique. We work both directions in the drill.

When we teach the cutoff block, we teach the three-step rule for the guards and a five-step rule for the tackles. Within three steps, the guards have to make a decision. They have to decide whether they can get leverage or they have to cut the defender. They come flat to the line of scrimmage to the inside. The guards take three steps and turn up, and the tackles take five steps and turn up.

We have some outstanding players in the offensive line. Chris Snee is always one step ahead of me in the drills. He is an outstanding player because he was well coached in college, and he wants to be the best lineman he can be. David Diehl has played everywhere on the offensive line except the center position. He can play center and has worked at that position. He played on the right side for McNally, but for most of his career, he has been a left tackle.

People keep saying he cannot play left tackle. He has two Super Bowl rings. When he played for Jim McNally, if we told him to step with the right foot, he wrote it down in his notes. I take his notes and type them up so I can remember what I said. If you give him a quiz on his assignments, it will be everything you said during the course of that week. You want player like that playing for you. He is unbelievable. We have other players who are bigger, quicker, and faster than he is, but he is better prepared than they are. I am not sure any of them are stronger than he is because he works his butt off in the weight room.

There are players all over this league who were fifth- and sixth-round picks who are first-round talents. David Diehl has first-round value for us as offensive lineman.

TECHNIQUE PRINCIPLES

- Eyes go to your landmark.
- Maintain knee bend.
- Keep chest on the thigh.
- Put weight on your insteps.
- Keep the elbows tight (hands squeeze the defender's rig cage).
- Aim your pads to your landmark.
- Hips should be behind your shoulders.
- Have knee drive; do not allow your feet to get beat.
- Finish with good (vertical) posture and explosion.

We want the weight on the insteps so we do not get top heavy. The eye level is under the pads of the defender. At our level, we do a lot of practice without pads. We do not put on the pads until we get to training camp. You learn to play the game with your hands and feet. However, we still play the game with the pads. You have to aim the pads at the landmark. The hips need to be behind the shoulders because you have more strength in your the legs and butt than the upper body. The hips and legs are essential when you block.

The hands are important, but the power comes from the lower body. If the feet stop, you are beat. You must have knee drive and finish. You must finish with good vertical posture and explosion.

I said it earlier, and I mean it. There are different ways of doing things. When I coach the rookies, I watch their feet. I can hear the punch on the sled or bags, but I watch the feet. I watch his footwork on the drive, reach, down, or combination blocks. If the feet continue to move after contact, there are two reasons for that. The player is physically bigger and stronger than the defender he is blocking, or his pad level is under the defender. If the blocker has to restart his feet, he does not have leverage on the defender.

If the feet stop and have to restart, the blocker does not have leverage. That is why we want to come off the ball and establish the leverage from the beginning. We want to maintain the foot movement and drive with the knees. At the end of the block, the blocker will gradually get taller in his posture. However, on the first step, we do not want the blocker to be tall. He starts out with his chest on his thighs and his finish is the same position.

DRILL WORK

We execute drills with a blocker and defender. The defender needs to align with proper leverage and give great effort. The objective of the drill is to simulate live blocking skills. You need to emphasis proper footwork, leverage, and finish. You need to tell your players why you are doing a particular drill and what you expect to get out of it.

I also believe the best drills you can do are the ones designed for the weakest players in your group. Do the drill for the players who need the work because he is not up to par with the rest of the group. Jim McNally has a drill for everything you would possibly need. Never do a drill just to do it.

REACH BLOCK: NORMAL AND WIDE 1-ON-1 BLOCKING

The first block is the reach block.

- *Objective:* Teach offensive linemen to explode with vertical leverage and to replace his second step on the ground with a good base (R.W.B.) versus a defender with horizontal alignment.
- *Footwork:* The first step creates a proper departure angle from the line of scrimmage. The first step is with the playside foot while getting the second step down (R.W.B.). The angle allows the blocker to keep his hips behind his shoulders, aim his pads to the landmark, and press his frontside shoulder.
- *Defender:* Bend with shield for leverage, and deliver a blow on contact.
- *Blocker:* Step with a good departure at an angle with vertical leverage and explosion with emphasis on getting the second step down (R.W.B.).

When we talk about the departure angle, it is important that the blocker does not get his hips turned to the sideline. He wants to press his frontside shoulder. When the blocker presses his frontside shoulder to square up, that gets his butt out of the hole. The departure angle adjusts to the width of the defender. If the defender is tight to the blocker, the angle is tighter. If he is wide, the angle is wider. The important thing is to get the second step on the ground because contact could happen on that step. The offensive lineman never wants to have one foot in the air on contact. On contact, the blocker wants both feet on the ground with a good base.

When we work the 1-on-1 reach block drill, I never want the center to take a rep without snapping the ball. In the first drill I showed you (what we call the demeanor drill), they do not snap the ball because there is no simulated blocking. In the 1-on-1 drill, I want them to do the two-step drill, punch, drive the knees, and finish the drill. The finish is a full arm extension pushing the shield up to a lock out position with the arms.

The next step is to take the drill work to the game. The play I want to show you is the weakside

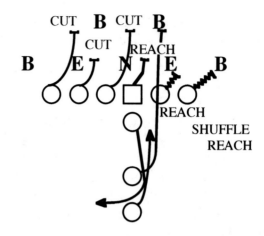

Diagram #2. Weakside Bob

Bob play (Diagram #2). To the weakside of the defense, the defenders align in a 3 technique on the guard and a wide 5 technique on the tackle. The inside linebackers are in 20 alignments on the offensive guard, and the nose plays a strongside angle on the center.

The right guard has a reach block on the 3 technique defender. He has to pound his feet and get the second step on the ground because the contact is coming on the second step. The offensive tackle has a defender in a two-point stance and is extremely wide. In some cases, the tackle may have to shuffle to the outside because the defender does not attack the line of scrimmage. They want to get their hats to the playside and finish their blocks.

The defender aligns in an outside technique and plays that gap responsibility. That means the ball is going inside the guard's block. The defender will try to escape the ball to the inside of the blocker. The blocker finishes his block with his inside knee and hand working up the inside of the defender.

The next block is the down block. The offensive blocker blocks back toward the ball. He has to block two types of defenders. He has to block the defender who is trying to penetrate and the one trying to cross face the blocker.

DOWN BLOCK

- Landmark: Near shoulder of the defender.
- Step with the near foot to the frontside of the near shoulder (second step down).

- Block your defender by turning your head up and in on the defender.
- Finish with your feet and pressure on the defender.

When we drill the down block, we align the defender on the line of scrimmage with the shield turned to the blocker (Diagram #3). The blocker aligns with his hand on the line of scrimmage. This puts the defender in the position he would be in if he came off the ball. All the defender has to do is meet force with force. When the blocker comes down on the shield, the defender meets force with force and works to cross face the blocker.

Diagram #3. Down Block

If the blocker has a down block versus a defender who is not penetrating, he changes his aiming point. He steps with the near foot, aiming for the backside of the near shoulder on his second step. The remaining parts of the technique are the same. He finishes with his feet and keeps pressure on the defender. When we drill this down block, the defender aligns two feet off the line of scrimmage with the shield turned toward the blocker. The blocker puts his hand on the line of scrimmage. The defender meets force with force and works to crossface the blocker. The blocker finishes with explosion and vertical leverage.

If the blocker cannot read by the defender's stance if he is trying to penetrate or play over the blocker, his target is the near shoulder. During the course of the game, the defense will adjust the way they play. The offensive lineman has to do the same thing. At some time during the game, he has to make a decision about what the defender is going to do. We want to make sure it is the right decision.

The center performs a down block when he blocks back for the pulling guard. He applies the same technique as a tackle blocking down on a 3 technique defender. He has to make a flat step to the line of scrimmage. The defender will try to grab the pulling guard to slow him down and keep him from pulling. If the center comes flat, he meets the defender on the line of scrimmage. He has to apply his rules and make the decision on the frontside or backside of the near shoulder. He steps flat, turns his head up and in, and finishes the block.

The footwork is to aim the first foot on the landmark and get the second step on the ground. They must maintain a good base with their feet. We say a good base is the feet at shoulder-width apart. Some players tend to get wider with their base, but they still can get the job done.

We use the down block on our toss play (Diagram #4). When you run the toss sweep, you must edge the defense at some point. Ideally, we want the tight end to seal the edge. In the diagram, we have a wing set and a double-team on the edge defender. If the tight end does not have a double-team blocker, it is hard for him to seal the edge. That is why the down block by the tackle on the 3 technique defender is so important. If the defensive end or outside linebacker plays outside on the tight end's block, the ballcarrier has to have a cutback. If the offensive tackle seals the 3 technique, the running back can cut it up and get positive yardage.

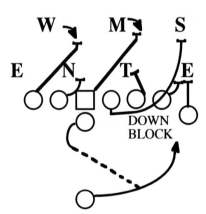

Diagram #4. Down Block Toss Sweep

We do not always go from a three-point stance. Occasionally, the offensive line will be in a two-point stance. The technique of the down block is the same from a two- or three-point stance, but you must drill in practice. When we put the quarterback in the shotgun, the offensive linemen are in two-point stances sometimes. We must be able to run the ball from the shotgun as well as from under the center. We must be able to run the ball from the two- or three-point stance.

In the two-point stance, the lineman puts his hands between the thigh boards and kneepads. He does not rest his elbows on his knees. We want him to be in an explosive position. I feel if the lineman starts with his elbows tight to his rib cage, it leads to a quicker punch. If the elbows in the two-point stance are outside, he has to move them to the inside to get into a position to deliver a blow. If the hands are up, the defender will chop them down as he comes off the ball.

COMBINATION BLOCK

We use combination-blocking techniques with adjacent linemen blocking a down linemen and linebacker with emphasis on moving the down lineman to the linebacker level. The covered offensive lineman is the post player, and the adjacent offensive lineman is the lead man.

POST BLOCKER

Take proper footwork to gain vertical leverage on the defender while giving the lead an area to hit on the defender. We execute this technique by moving the inside foot in relationship to the defender's horizontal leverage. We get vertical leverage, allowing the lead man to work with him. He must give the lead man something to hit to get movement on the down defender.

Move the foot away from the lead man. This initial step depends on the alignment of the defender. When the defender is in a head-up alignment, the first step is a lateral step with the second step to the landmark of the inside of the near knee of the defender. If the defender has a horizontal alignment, the post player's first step is a pick-up-and-put-down step in order to close the space with the lead man while the second step to the landmark of the inside of the near knee of the defender.

That means the post blocker is going to close the space between him and the lead blocker. He never works out to the lead blocker. The lead block steps to the post blocker. If the defender has horizontal leverage, the post man picks up his inside foot and puts it down (Diagram #5). He gets his second step on the ground and works to the landmark of the inside knee of the defender.

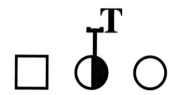

Diagram #5. Horizontal Alignment

The next situation is the post player with a head-up alignment by the defender (Diagram #6). With the defender head-up, the post blocker takes a lateral step with his inside foot to give the lead blocker something to hit. The length of the step must accomplish that goal.

Diagram #6. Head-Up Alignment

LEAD BLOCKER

Step with your near foot to the post man. This footwork is lateral to the defender's near number as a landmark. Work your knees, hips, and shoulders square to the defender. This allows you to move the defender off the line of scrimmage and gain hip-to-hip leverage with the post man.

This is the place you can get different points of view in the combination block. What I am going to tell you is what we do at the New York Giants. If the lead man takes a lead step to the inside with his inside foot, he works against the post blocker. We teach a lateral step down the line of scrimmage with the inside foot. The second step follows down the line, and the third step is up the field.

By the time the third step hits the ground, I want the inside knee perpendicular to the line of scrimmage (Diagram #7). If the knee turns to the inside, the lead man has a tendency to step underneath himself with his third step. We do not want that to happen. We coach for that not to happen, but they still do it. They may be a little bow-legged, are not as good an athlete, or do not understand the technique. You have to work to get the proper footwork. They must get the knees in

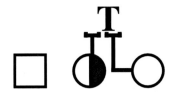

Diagram #7. Lead Player Step

the proper place because that aligns the hips and the hips align the shoulders.

This technique works. It gets the players to the place they need to go. We as coaches will give the players parameters to do it. With the defender in a horizontal alignment, the post player's second step has to be at the inside of the defender's outside leg or in the crotch of the defender. The post blocker has to get vertical leverage on the defender by getting his pads under the pads of the defender. If the post player does not get his pads under the pads of the defender, it is difficult for the lead blocker to get movement. The post blocker makes that common mistake.

The problem with the lead blocker is working against the post blocker. Instead of working with the post blocker, he squeezes against him and forces him inside. That mistake occurs when the lead blocker's inside knee goes toward the defender instead of laterally to the inside.

When you coach, you explain the principles of the block. The players understand where to go and what to do, and then you execute the block. The follow-up is correcting the mistakes in the execution. We want the post and lead blockers working together, not against one another. If the blockers work against one another, the defenders split the block.

The combination block takes the down linemen to the second level with one blocker coming off for a linebacker. The way we describe the block is: four hands on the down lineman and four eyes on the linebacker. One of the blockers overtakes the down lineman, and one will come off for the linebacker. The block on the linebacker will depend on where he tries to fill. If he plays over the top of the combination, the lead blocker takes the linebacker, and the post man blocks the down lineman. If the linebacker plays under the combination block, the post player blocks the linebacker, and the lead blocker blocks the down man.

When we run a frontside combination block, we want to get the defender on one foot. The defender reads the double-team and drops his outside shoulder toward the lead blocker. The coaching point for the lead blocker as he laterally steps inside is to get his inside pad under the outside pad of the defender. The lead blocker cannot allow the defender to stay in the hole. He has to bend his knees, get his near pad under the near pad of the defender, and drive him vertically.

If the defender stunts outside, we have no trouble handling that (Diagram #8). With the down defender in a horizontal alignment, the post player is picking up and putting down his inside foot. When the defender slants to the outside, the post player allows the lead blocker to take on that block, and he stays on his track to the inside.

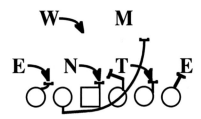

Diagram #8. Combination vs. Movement

The footwork in the combination block has to be good to keep the lead blocker from stepping on the post blocker's feet. That rarely ever occurs because they know where the other lineman will place his feet. They both understand where the other player is going to step.

On a combination block, the center, guard, tackle, or tight end can be the post blocker or lead blocker, depending on the play. If the tight end has a wing set outside of him, he can be the post blocker with the wing as the lead blocker. When you do the drill work, that is the approach you must use. You work down the line using post techniques and lead techniques. When you work your chute drills, use the post and lead footwork in the chute.

The player you must work hard on getting the footwork is the center. It is hard for the center to pick his foot up and set it down without stepping back off the line of scrimmage. The offensive linemen at our level can play up and down the line of scrimmage. The techniques are the same from any position. They know their assignments, they also know their teammate's assignments, and can play his position. You must drill the technique, execute the techniques, and correct the techniques repeatedly.

Pass Blocking Progression (Two-Point)

- The stance should be balanced and explosive.
- Place the heel of the hand between the thigh board and the kneepad. Align your elbows tight to the rib cage.
- Set the feet to block your defender from an inside-out position.

Pocket Integrity

Protect the pass from an inside-out position. Keep the defender between the blocker and the passer.

UNDERSTANDING THE PROTECTION

- How many protectors (five-, six-, seven-, and eight-man protection)?
- How many steps is the quarterback dropping back?
- Where is the quarterback's launch point?

The one thing the offensive lineman needs to know is how to protect the passer. You have someone dropping back who is defenseless. If you hand the ball to the running back, he has the chance to make someone miss if the lineman misses a block. If you miss a block in pass protection because you do not know what you are doing, that is not good. That gets me fired, and has everybody on the bus going in the wrong direction. If we get #10 hurt because we miss a block, it is bad for everyone.

If we use a five-man protection, there is no running back or tight end blocking in the scheme. We need to know where the quarterback is dropping. Is it the inside leg of the frontside guard or the inside leg of the frontside tackle? If it is a five-step drop, the quarterback will behind the center. If we call "Max," the quarterback's drop is a seven-step drop. If the quarterback says "Firm," it is a three-step drop. We must know where he will be in the pocket.

The tackles create and maintain the width of the pocket (Diagram #9). The center and guards create and maintain the depth of the pocket. The depth allows the quarterback to step up into the pocket. We have too many protections in our scheme; however, we have to understand them all. We must understand to whom we are sliding. If we have a four-man rush, we must know who the uncovered lineman will be.

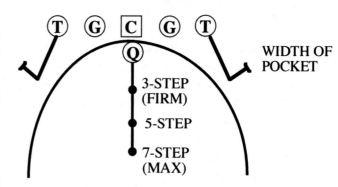

Diagram #9. Pocket Integrity

If the lineman is uncovered, he is looking for work. It is important for the uncovered lineman to know where to find the work. If the defense is a three-man front, the tackles and center are covered. The two guards are uncovered. If they do not know where to find work, you will have the center and two guards beating the hell out of the nose tackle while the two offensive tackles are fighting for their lives against a speed rushing defender.

In our protection scheme, we generally have a running back working with the protection scheme. Against the three-man rush, if the running back aligns to the left side of the formation, we call right. That tells the running back he helps the left tackle on the defensive end. The left uncovered guard works with the center on the nose tackle. The right offensive guard works with the right tackle on the defensive end. Define where the uncovered linemen help in your scheme. Do not make it a random choice.

Dan Dierdorf said, "Pass blocking is like a precise dance step; it has to be precise time after time. There is only one way I know to be sure. That is, you have to study yourself every day." I believe what Dan said. These players have been through the wars and have done the pass blocking.

We do a number of different footwork drills. We drill the line sets. We have a normal set, vertical set, wide set, and a play-action pass set. The lineman has to set his feet between the quarterback and the pass rusher. The move vulnerable rush is the inside rush. When we do our sets, we want to give the defender one-way to go, and that is to the outside.

We do pass protection punch drills. The first thing we teach is the hand placement on the punch. We want them to punch into the pectoral area of the rusher. We punch with an upward motion. We do not want to punch at a level or downward movement. If you do that, it causes a bend at the waist. When we punch, we want to snap the heel of the hand to redirect the rusher. The terms we use repeatedly are catch, bench, and press.

At the New York Giants practice facility, we have a cruncher sled. We punch the sled instead of pads.

CRUNCHER SLED DRILLS

- *Alternate punch:* Lineman executes three punches with leverage as he slides to every other pad on the sled.
- *Cross punch:* Lineman executes a cross punch as he slides to alternate pads.
- *Wide set punch:* The lineman aligns on the pad to simulate a wide rusher. On command, he sets and jams the edge of the pad with his outside hand while keeping his outside shoulder as square as possible. Alternate punch with outside and inside hand.
- *Power set punch:* The lineman aligns on the pad to simulate an inside rusher. On command, he sets and jams the edge of the pad with his inside hand while keeping his inside shoulder as square as possible. Alternate punch with inside and outside hand.

That allows our players to punch the crap out of the sleds, and no one has to hold anything for them. The sled has a little spring to it. There are many ways to practice the punch, but that is how we do it. The centers use the cross punch. They snap the ball with their right hand and cross punch with the left hand. When we work the punch drills, we work them in sequences of three punches. On the power set, we punch inside, outside, and inside punches.

We use the medicine ball in our punch drill. The medicine ball is 23 inches in diameter and weighs 19 pounds. We do a drill called hot potato. The players are in a two-point stance with their right foot up. The partner tosses the ball to the blocker. The blocker punches the ball back to his partner. The partner must toss the ball high so the blocker does not have to punch level or down at the ball. We do the drill with the right foot up and repeat it with the left foot up.

We use a drill called the half-moon drill. Four players are positioned in a semi-circle. There is an offensive player in the middle with three defenders holding medicine ball in front of him and to his right and left. The blocker sets on the player in front of him and punches the ball. Then, he sets on the angle of his position and punches that ball. He finishes the drill by setting the opposite direction and punching that ball.

The third type of drill is the toss and punch drill. The blocker works with a partner. They shuffle right and left, tossing and punching the ball. They shuffle at a 45-degree angle tossing and punching the ball. The third thing they do is shuffle in a circle tossing and punching the ball.

The thing about tossing the ball is keeping the hands tight and ready to punch. If you are not ready, the ball will break through the hands and hit you in the nose. The partners are two to three yards apart. To punch the ball back, the players has to bend his knees and use power in his legs and arms to get the ball back. They need the hands together and punch with the heel to get the ball back to the partner.

It is important for the blocker to keep his chin back and always punch up on the ball. If he punches level or down, he tips forward. We want the chin and shoulders back and punching up at an angle. That is the posture of pass protection.

PLAY-ACTION PASS

The play-action pass is a pass, which comes off a running play. The first one I want to show you comes off the sprint 38 play. We tag the play and call "sprint 238 Max," which is the play-action off the 38 play (Diagram #10). Everything on the play should look and sound the same as the run. The

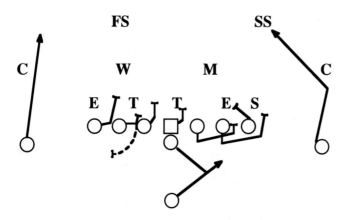

Diagram #10. Sprint 238 Max

quarterback makes the fake and sets up in the C gap. It is an eight-man protection scheme. The running back making the fake is responsible for the fourth man coming from the playside.

To your young players, you must define what "look and sound like run" means. The safety keys the tight end. If the tight end blocks down, he looks at the linemen for a secondary key. He is looking for a high hat or a pass protection set. If the linemen's pads are down in a run-blocking scheme, he is on the way to the line of scrimmage.

In our league, when you tell the tight end to pass protect on a defensive end, it could be trouble. They pay the tight end to run routes, catch the ball, and block linebackers in the run game. They do not pay him to pass protect against defensive end. However, we ask him to do it. We tell the guard as he comes around to help the tight end if he needs help. The guard is looking for work, but he knows where to look. He knows his assignment and knows the assignment of the tight end. He pulls for the Mike linebacker. If the Mike linebacker reads the play and drops, the guard helps the tight end.

To the backside of the play, the guard and tackle on the running play work a backside combination block for the down defender and the Will linebacker. If the Will linebacker reads the play, the tackle peels back and helps the second tight end with the defensive end. We call that move a pirouette. If for some reason the down defender went to the tackle, the guard peels out to help the tight end. When they pirouette back they turn over their inside shoulder. They move to the inside, turn over the inside shoulder, and peel back. By turning off the inside shoulder, he gets the correct depth and have a continuous flow.

Since the play is an eight-man Max protection, the linemen know the quarterback is in a seven-step drop. However, sometimes the seven-step drop ends up in a 10-step drop, which amazes me.

The weakside zone play is 37 sprint Zorro. The play-action pass is ride 337 Max base (Diagram #11). We can run the route from a twin or triple set. I am not going to talk about the routes. I am going to talk about the protection. We fake the 37 zone play and bring the quarterback to the outside leg of the backside guard in a seven-step drop. The defense in the diagram is a 4-2-5 under front. To the weakside, we block down with the tackle and pull the guard for the defensive end. We call that "gee-it."

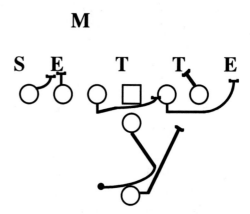

Diagram #11. Ride 337 Max Base

Since the launch point is the outside leg of the backside guard, the offensive line wants to prevent the defense from getting to that area. We want to zone the backside in our protection. We call that a "zone-it." We want to block the play-action like the run.

If we feel we are going see a blitz, we have a call to take us out of the scheme blocking protection. That means we are zone blocking the play instead of blocking it like the running play. We do not pull anyone.

Another example of how we could block the defense uses a center pull to the weakside. On the backside of the play, the tight end has to block the defensive end. The backside tackle comes down into the B gap and helps the guard. However, if the linebacker reads the play and retreats, the tackle uses

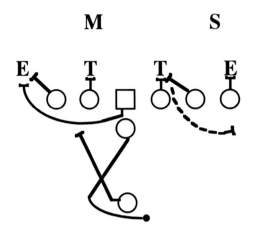

Diagram #12. Pirouette

the pirouette move and peels back to help the tight end trying to block the defensive end (Diagram #12).

The tackle moves to the inside, finds no one there, pirouettes over his inside shoulder, and intercepts the rushing defensive end at the proper depth. The center can pull to the outside or help the offensive guard to the weakside.

I know I jumped around some, but here is what I tried to do today. Whatever you do as far as teaching the stance is up to you. Do whatever works for you, and believe in it. Be prepared, and never stand in front of your players and coaches if you are not sure of what you are talking about or believe. When you prepare for a meeting, make sure you cover all the bases and know what you are presenting.

When we talk about moving players against their will from one place to another, make sure you know how to teach it so they can execute. There are different ways to do the same thing. Use what works best for you to teach your players.

The game of football is still a leverage game. It is pad under pad and moving people in whatever direction you want to move them. I want to move the players back, but moving a player from point A to point B may be a lateral movement. How we get the movement involves knowing the proper landmark. Remember, they have to bend their knees and get their chest on their thighs with their eyes on the landmark.

Step to the landmark and get the second down on the ground. We know how to coach those things, and we do it repeatedly. We do not get too concerned with the X's and O's in our game. We teach and coach the reach, down, and combination blocks as our staple.

When you feel like you are doing too much on offense, cut it back. Make sure you teach the fundamentals and use the same explosive stance every time you align. We need to keep it fundamental and not be so sophisticated in the approach. This is a great game, and you guys do a great job of coaching it. My hat is off to you coaches. You take the youngsters from square one and give them the building blocks they need to build the foundation.

With all the things that are going on in the NFL as related to concussions, I want to say this is the greatest game there ever was. It is better than any other sport out there. I grew up the son of a high school coach. He coached until the day he died. That is all I have ever known. When I was in college, he asked me what I wanted to do when I graduated. I told him I wanted to coach. He told me I had to be crazy to want that. I told him that was all I wanted to do.

This is a great profession. However, remember, we teach it safety first. That is our job. When I talk to the linemen I coach before we put helmets on, I talk about the safety of the neck. What I tell them is simple, but it is true and it works. I tell them to put their chin up and their mouths open. I tell them their neck muscles are supporting the spinal cord. I have them put their left ear on their left shoulder. When they do that, the neck is not in a supportive position for the spinal cord. That means the spinal cord is vulnerable to injury. I have the put their right ear on the right shoulder, the head back, and the head forward. In those positions, the spinal cord is exposed.

I tell them to not turn their head or duck their head because they will put the spinal cord in a vulnerable position. That is important to us as teachers of this game. I believe that. The other thing I tell them is to get their feet out of the hole. I tell them that because we want to open holes, but at the same time, I do not want someone clipping them from the backside. You see it all the time, when offensive linemen are rolled up from behind accidently in the wash of the play.

Football is a hard sport. It is a physical sport. Moreover, it is a collision sport. However, the game has not changed over the years. The thing that remains constant in this game is the coaches. It is how you teach the game from a safety and sportsmanship type of concept. I congratulate you coaches, and thanks for putting up with me today.

ABOUT THE AUTHOR

Pat Flaherty, who has more than 30 years of coaching experience, is in his 12th season as an NFL coach and eighth as the Giants' offensive line coach.

The Giants have consistently had one of the NFL's best and most dependable offensive lines during Flaherty's tenure. The team's offense has been ranked among the top eight in the NFL in each of the last three years, and the Giants have had at least two linemen selected to the Pro Bowl in each of those seasons. Five players—center Shaun O'Hara, guards Chris Snee and Rich Seubert, and tackles David Diehl and Kareem McKenzie—have been mainstays on the line the last four seasons. The group started 38 consecutive regular season games from 2007 to 2009, then the only such streak by five linemen since the 1970 NFL merger.

In 2010, Snee and O'Hara were each selected to the Pro Bowl for the third consecutive year (O'Hara was unable to play in the game because of an injury). O'Hara and Snee are the first Giants offensive linemen selected to three Pro Bowls since center Bart Oates in 1990, 1991, and 1993 and the first chosen in three consecutive years since Hall of Famer tackle Rosie Brown was selected to six in a row from 1955 to 1960.

With the line playing at a high level, the Giants were fifth in the NFL with an average of 380.3 yards a game. They gained a franchise-record 6,085 yards, the first 6,000-yard season in their history. The Giants were one of only two teams with a pair of backs who rushed for more than 800 yards apiece in Ahmad Bradshaw (1,235 yards) and Brandon Jacobs (823), and the Giants tied the Indianapolis Colts by allowing an NFL-low 16 sacks in 2010. That was easily the fewest sacks allowed by the Giants since the 16-game season was instituted in 1978. Their previous low total was 24 sacks allowed in 2002. The Giants did not allow a sack in a franchise-record five consecutive games (November 7 through December 5) and in seven games overall.

The line registered these accomplishments despite a spate of injuries that forced Flaherty to start six different offensive line combinations. The Giants started three left tackles (Diehl, Shawn Andrews, and Will Beatty), three left guards (Seubert, Diehl, and Kevin Boothe), and three centers (O'Hara, Adam Koets, and Seubert).

Snee, the right guard, and right tackle Kareem McKenzie started all 16 games at the same position. Seubert also started 16 games—nine at left guard and seven at center, though he suffered a knee injury in the season finale at Washington that forced Boothe to play center.

In 2009, O'Hara, Snee, and Diehl all played in the Pro Bowl, the first time the Giants had three players from the same position group play in the game since 1962.

The previous year, Snee and O'Hara were selected to the NFC Pro Bowl team. Snee, who was a starter, was the first Giants guard to play in the Pro Bowl since Stone in 2001, and O'Hara was the first Giants center to go to the game since Bart Oates in 1993. In addition, Diehl was selected as a third alternate.

With the line leading the way, the Giants that season rushed for NFL-leading and franchise-record numbers of 2,518 yards and 5.0 yards per carry. It was the first time since 1993 that the Giants led the NFL in rushing.

In 2007, the line was an important factor as the Giants finished fourth in the NFL in rushing yardage with 134.3 yards a game. The Giants were also fourth in the league with a 4.6 yards-per-carry average. In 2006, the Giants were seventh in the NFL with an average of 134.8 rushing yards a game and sixth with an average of 4.7 yards per carry. The Giants' 138.1-yard rushing average in 2005 placed them sixth in the league. In 2004, the Giants averaged 119.0 yards a game and 4.5 yards per carry, which were far superior to the 97.4 and 4.0 averages the Giants posted in 2003, the year before Tom Coughlin and Flaherty arrived.

The Giants had a 1,000-yard rusher in six of the first seven seasons in which Flaherty coached the line. In 2008, Jacobs (1,089) and Derrick Ward (1,025) became just the fourth set of running back teammates in NFL history with more than 1,000 rushing yards in the same season. In 2007, Jacobs rushed for 1,009 yards, despite missing five games and most of a sixth with injuries. Tiki Barber made the only three Pro Bowls of his career while rushing for 1,518, 1,860, and 1,662 yards in the three years he ran behind a Flaherty-coached line.

Prior to joining the Giants, Flaherty was the Chicago Bears' tight ends coach for three seasons. Under Flaherty, the group was instrumental in helping Anthony Thomas twice rush for more than 1,000 yards, including 1,024 yards in 2003. In addition, Chicago's tight ends played a bigger role in the team's passing attack under Flaherty. In 2003, Desmond Clark caught 44 passes, the third-highest total on the Bears.

In 2000, Flaherty coached the Washington Redskins' tight ends and helped Stephen Alexander earn an invitation to the Pro Bowl. Alexander was third on the Redskins that season with 47 catches.

Flaherty began his coaching career at his alma mater, DeLone Catholic High School, in McSherrytown, Pennsylvania, from 1978 to 1980.

Flaherty coached in the collegiate ranks from 1980 to 1999. He began with a two-year stint coaching the offensive line at East Stroudsburg University, his alma mater. Flaherty joined the staff at Penn State University in 1982, a season in which the Nittany Lions defeated Georgia in the Sugar Bowl to win the national championship. After two seasons at Penn State, Flaherty moved to Rutgers University, where he coached the offensive line for eight years.

Flaherty spent the 1992 season coaching the defensive line at East Carolina. From 1993 to 1998, he was on the staff at Wake Forest University, where he coached the offensive line, tight ends, and special teams. In 1999, he coached tight ends and special teams and was in charge of recruiting at the University of Iowa.

Flaherty was an All-America center at East Stroudsburg. He was inducted into the school's Hall of Fame in October 2004. He and his wife, Lynne, have two children, Shawn and Colleen.

Jim McNally

LOSING GROUND, TIPPING, A GAP ENTRIES, AND BLOCKING TIPS

Cincinnati Bengals

Gentlemen, it is a pleasure to be here. I think conditioning is important in anything you do. When you do anything with your players, I think you need to put them in a bent-knee position and make them move around. I am 68 years old, and I think I am in decent shape. I am not bragging. I think if you put your players in the bent-knee position and do the duck demeanor movement, it can be a good conditioner tool.

To get into that position, you bend your knees with your toes outside. That brings the knees to the inside slightly with the weight on the inside of your feet. Staying in that position and moving the feet for as little as 10 minutes can be a great conditioner for offensive linemen. I wanted to show you that because it applies to linemen conditioning and is applicable to their techniques.

I want to show you one thing that none of us do. You can say you do it, but you really do not. The player's feet must always move. Watch the end of a drill or the end of a play and see what the player's feet are doing. The player who keeps his feet moving is the one who is blocking people.

When I taught pass blocking, I used to teach a kick-slide and a power-post step to the inside. I do not teach that anymore. I teach pass blockers to move their feet at all time to change their position. They can use the demeanor steps to move inside as well as outside. When we engage and hit and make contact, the feet cannot stop moving. I do not believe we emphasize the point to keep the feet moving even when we stop the directional movement. I learned that in the seventh grade. The feet are always on the ground, and always moving. When I first started teaching pass blocking, we moved at a deliberate pace and did not keep the feet moving at all times.

Moving the feet in a rapid movement allows me to change directions quickly. If I am moving outside in a deliberate manner and there is a need to change directions and get to the inside, I cannot do it quickly unless my feet are already moving.

We all know that long steps in a blocking technique lead to failure. If you listen to the foot movement of your players, you should hear the short, choppy movement steps. You should not hear a stomp followed by a sliding or scraping sound of the feet being dragged along the ground. You should hear a constant tapping of the feet in a short, choppy movement. It does not matter at what level you play. The tighter the feet, the faster you can change direction. Tight means the feet do not go very far when the player is moving.

I started doing the duck demeanor technique in 1978. My friend at Penn State University improved on it somewhat. Instead of pumping the arms up and down with the foot movement, he put his hands together and rolled a tennis ball in them. That put his hands up and kept his elbows into his rib cage, as you would do in blocking. The duck demeanor movement gave him the footwork, and the tennis ball rolling simulated the hand action in blocking.

I heard Damian Wroblewski from Rutgers University speak at one of these clinics, and he talked about deep breathing. I do not know the exact timing of the exercise, but it happens just before you strike a blow. Just before you hit or strike a blow, you bark out a sound. The bark is a sound that projects a punch. It is like a weight lifter screaming out a strain as he completes a lift. I found myself, when I would demonstrate a technique, barking out a sound as I simulated each repetition in the demonstration.

I did not quite understand what he was talking about until I started to think about it. I think the bark occurs after the second step in run or close order blocking. You take the first step, get the second foot on the ground, and then "Whoop" (grunt or straining sound) you make the hit. It gives you more explosion and thrust when you let out that air when you are breathing. If you encourage your players to exhale and make that barking noise on the hit and strikes in your drill, it could help them.

I listened to Mike Solari speak, and I liked his idea about using the forearms in the double-under move. To gain leverage in a block, we use a technique called a double-under move. The objective of the move is to lift the defender by getting the hands into the belt area of the defender and lifting him while keeping the knees in a bent position. You do not want to take the bend out of the legs. We do not want the blocker to stand up. We want to lift the defender with his forearms and hands.

To keep them from standing up, we do a drill called the "turtle drill" (Diagram #1). This is a simple drill. The players face one another one yard apart. The blocker puts his hands behind his back and bends as low as he can. We want his head up and his back arched. The partner assumes the same posture opposite him. On the command, the blocker takes his first and second step in his blocking sequence. On the second step, his head comes forward and pops his partner on the trademark area of the headgear. It is like a turtle poking his head out of his shell.

want to establish leverage and maintain control of the defender. We must hit on the rise.

The footwork on the double-under is important. If the guard has to block a 3 technique defender, his first step has to lower his center of gravity. We used to step forward on the first step, but that locked the hips of the linemen. The first step is a more lateral step than forward to lower the center of gravity and get the lineman down. It is not a backward step.

When linemen strike on most blocks, they gather themselves. It is almost like a pause before the strike. When the lineman comes out at a linebacker, before he strikes he gathers himself and delivers the blow. The first step lowers the center of gravity and the second step is lower than the first.

Coaches do not do much of what I call the "cross-shove" (Diagram #2). If we run the inside zone play, it goes up the middle. The running back aligns at seven yards deep, and his aiming point is the butt of the center. If the center has a noseguard aligned in a head-up position, the center and backside guard work a zone block for the nose and the backside linebacker.

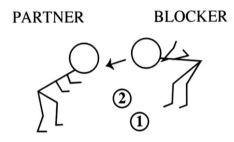

Diagram #1. Turtle Drill

The objective of the drill is to make the blocker understand that he does not have to stand up to do the double-under lift. He has to keep the knees bent and get under the defender. The double-under drill trains the hands to get under the defender and create leverage.

No longer are offensive line coaches teaching a total flat back in blocking. If you teach that, the defender will olé the blocker and make the tackle. The running backs are seven to eight yards deep, and the contact in the blocks has to last longer. We

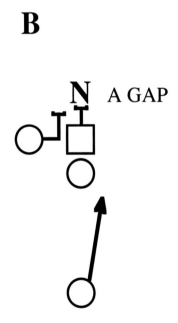

Diagram #2. Cross-Shove

The backside guard is in a left-handed stance. The linebacker has a head-up alignment on him. To execute the zone block, the guard does not need to take a lead zone step to the center because the center is not going to reach the noseguard. The center comes off square to the line of scrimmage at the nose and engages into a drive block. That means there is not as much gray area in the gap between the center and backside guard. The backside guard uses a high-leg cross-shuffle technique. He steps with his inside foot and shuffles to the inside keeping his inside leg high.

The running back presses the A gap, and the guard shuffles down the line of scrimmage instead of lead stepping into the nose. He takes two quick shuffle steps to the inside and closes the gap between the center and him. If the nose hangs in the gray area on the backside of the center, the backside guard uses his hands and shoves the nose back onto the center's block. After he shoves the nose back onto the center's block, he moves up to the linebacker.

The nose likes to play the backside gap on the zone play so he frees up the backside linebacker. The guard prevents him from playing the backside by putting him back on the center's block. You do not want the center trying to turn the nose to the backside because his butt is in the hole if he does. We want the center to stay square on the nose and react to his movement if he goes to the frontside of the play.

If the nose goes to the playside of the zone play, the center blocks him that way and the ball breaks to the backside. If the nose goes to the backside, the guard puts him back on the center's block and goes up to the linebacker. The guard takes his two shuffle steps to the inside and shoves across his body with the outside hand to put the nose back on the center's block (Diagram #3). He does not turn his shoulders to the inside to make the shove. He must stay square so he can recoil to the outside if the defensive tackle spikes from the outside.

This is a situation where the guard does not have to lead or bucket step to make the zone block. He can shuffle to the center because the center is not trying to reach the nose. The center's block is a straight drive block because the running back goes straight ahead. If we know we are going to use this type of technique, the guard wants to crowd the ball. That allows the guard to go sideways with a high inside leg and jack the nose back onto the center's block.

Another example of where we can use this technique is to the backside against a 3 technique defender (Diagram #4). The backside formation has a tight end to that side. The defensive alignments are a 3 and 7 technique by the down linemen and a stack linebacker over the defensive end. In that situation, we know the linebacker is not going to fill across the 3 technique defender. However, we could get the 7 technique defender on a spike to the inside.

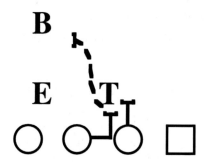

Diagram #4. 3 Technique Defender

We want to work the zone block on the 3 technique defender to the backside linebacker. The offensive tackle uses the cross-shove technique on the 3 technique before he goes up to the linebacker. He does not need to zone-step to the inside to try to overtake the 3 technique. He knows the ball is going up the middle, and the linebacker is not going to play over the top of the 3 technique defender. He knows there could be the spike from the 7 technique defender. It is the same situation for him, and he can react back to the spike.

We do not use high-leg shuffle techniques only on double-team blocks. We can use them on the

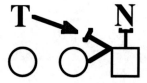

Diagram #3. Defensive Tackle Spike

backside of zone blocks. We can use it on the frontside of an inside zone play (Diagram #5). There are times that the lead foot can be forward in the technique, if we align in a wing set to the tight end. If we want the playside tackle and tight end to block the 7 technique and Sam linebacker, we can use the same technique.

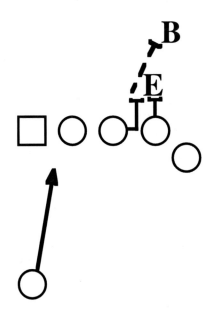

Diagram #5. Frontside Technique

The playside tackle can use the high-leg shuffle to put the 7 technique defender back on the tight end's block before moving up to block the Sam linebacker. The ball goes up the middle. The tackle keeps his shoulder square, and has a high outside leg.

When we use an overtake technique, we call it "overlap." The problem with the overtake block is the uncovered blocker coming inside. Too many times, he knocks the inside blocker off the block (Diagram #6). When you run the zone scheme with an overtake technique, the uncovered lineman has

Diagram #6. Overlap

to overlap the inside blocker. The backside blocker takes his bucket step to the inside and gets his backside shoulder across the defender's backside pad. He does not come flat to the line of scrimmage with his helmet in the inside blocker's back. He wants to position himself behind the blocker, working up to the second level.

The overtake blocker cannot push the inside blocker off the block. It will help him get to his block on the linebacker, but it pushes him off-balance. He has to overlap the inside blocker by getting the proper depth on the first and second steps.

Every block must have a finish. When the lineman uses the double-under technique, he has to finish the block. At the end of a block when you feel yourself getting too high, there is a simple technique that can help. When the blocker feels he is starting to get too high on his block, he can hop back and restart his drive. It is the same technique as if a pass rusher is overwhelming the blocker. When he hops back, he lowers his center of gravity and recaptures the leverage of the block. That allows him to restart and gives him the secondary finish to the block.

The blocker is actually losing some ground, but he regains the momentum to finish the block. Make that a part of your drill work. While I am talking about drills, let me encourage you to make the drill work things that happen in the game.

I think the best way to drill is to drill what happens in the game. As coaches, we have to coach the players on techniques. However, the best way to drill is to block man-on-man. It does not have to be a full-speed drill. What it has to be is a real person and not a blocking dummy. When you do a board drill, the linemen block a bag down the board for 10 yards. That is not what happens in the game. Coaches love drills. They are time taker-uppers. They always look for more drills. The drills you want to do are the ones that happen in the game.

The drills are not weaving in and out of the bags or forward rolls. You train the techniques then drill the techniques against live players. Do all the other things during the off-season. When the season starts, drill football. Train them to block on the Crowther sled and whatever else you need to train them. After that, drill your techniques and assignments in football drills. The individual periods are for the center and guards working their combination block on the nose and backside linebacker. Do not wait until team drills to teach those techniques. Do it right from the get-go.

I see a problem with teams that run the stretch zone play. The play I am talking about is the play that stretches to the tight end position. I am not talking about the wide stretch that Indianapolis runs two yards outside the tight end. Coaches teach the linemen to get their heads to the outside of the defenders so they widen the defender. There is no play if the defender two gaps the blocker and comes straight ahead.

In my opinion, any play that goes from the tight end to the guard, the correct block is to turn the defenders outside. You eventually block the defender, but we want to turn him out rather than try to reach him. I call that "tipping the defenders." The blocker uses the momentum of the defender to turn him out and the ball cuts up inside. The only time the ball goes outside is when the defenders pinch to the inside.

If we run a mid-zone play where the ball is going between the guard and tight end, we want to use a tipping block (Diagram #7). We do not give up the inside to the defender. We attack on a 45-degree angle to the outside. We want to stop penetration and create movement to the outside. However, we try to tip the defender to the outside and let the ball cut back inside the blockers. The blocker uses his inside hand on the defender to turn him outside and let the ball cut back. Using this technique, the linemen have a good base and their feet do not get crossed.

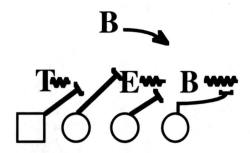

Diagram #7. Tipping the Stretch

If the ball is going extremely wide, you cannot use this technique. You may have to use a jump-turn technique to reach the defender. You may have to block down and pull around. What cannot happen is for the linemen to get flatten out at the line of scrimmage.

I want to go back and review some of the things that I talked about. In run blocking, the first step lowers the center of gravity. However, it is not a forward step. His first step does not go forward, but his body does not go backward. With the first step, the body is going forward and the blocker is lowering his center of gravity.

If the blocker steps forward, it puts him on a tightrope. His second step crosses over and causes him to be off-balance. In this technique, all the first step is trying to do is lower the center of gravity and get the hips out of the way so the second step can get on the ground. He picks up his foot and places it in a lateral position to the outside. When he strikes, both feet are on the ground. When the blocker engages the defender, he cannot simply run off the ball. He takes his two-step start and gathers himself before he strikes.

I want to talk about a mid-zone play. It does not matter if the play is a run to the strongside or to the weakside. The running back steps are not important. He can drop-step or step opposite the play. What is important is the angle of his shoulders. His shoulders are not square.

They point at his aiming point. The aiming point could be in the inside leg of the tight end or the outside leg of the tackle. It could be the inside leg of the tackle. They are all the same to me. He is running toward the C gap with his shoulders on an angle. In my opinion, between the tight end and the guard you should have only one zone play.

When the back attacks the line of scrimmage with his shoulder square to the line, it presents a problem for the linemen. If the ball cuts back, the defenders fall back into the play and the blockers look like crap. When the back turns his pads on an angle, the linebackers move. You can call the play a four- or six-hole play because it is the same play. I run the play from the butt of the guard to the inside leg of the tight end. Mid-zone blocking is a stretch play, but it is not a wide play.

The New York Jets have the best center in the NFL. He is about 6'5" and weighs about 330 pounds.

He is as strong as an ox. Tony Wise worked with him, and Bill Callahan and I worked with him at the Jets. His only problem was he was a little stiff in the ankles. The first year we started working with him, we taught him this technique.

I was doing the double-under and high-leg gallop in 1999, and everyone laughed at me. I told them they could laugh all they wanted because 10 years later it would be the newest stuff in the business.

We had to teach the center to block the shade noseguard. If the center tried to reach the nose, the nose flattens him out at the line of scrimmage. If the nose aligns in a 1 technique or 2i technique on the guard, we want the center to block him. However, he has to snap the ball and is the closest lineman to the line of scrimmage (Diagram #8). If he snaps the ball and comes off at an angle to the nose, he cannot block him. We wanted the center to come off on an angle so he overlapped the guard.

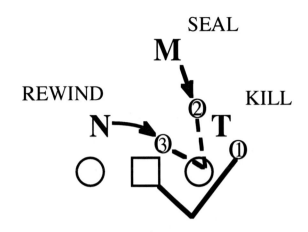

Diagram #9. Three Options

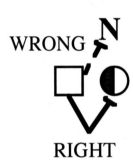

Diagram #8. Center Overlap

There are three things the center can do using that angle off the line of scrimmage (Diagram #9). He can overtake the noseguard, he can move up on the linebacker, or he can rewind and strike backside if the entire defensive line slanted to the playside. Using this angle, he can work with the guard on a 3 technique defender. He has a decision to make. He can kill or overtake the 3 technique. He can work up to the linebacker, if he blows the A gap, or he can rewind back to the 1 technique slant to the playside.

We call the technique a "bracer-skip" step. The playside foot comes off the line of scrimmage in what everyone calls a brace step. Since we wanted the step to be deeper and wider than the brace step, we termed it a bracer step. The second step in the movement is the skip step. We open the hips to get the deep reach or bracer step off the line of scrimmage. The skip step slides along the ground to balance the base. After the skip, the third step is with the inside foot on the proper angle.

When the center takes the bracer-skip step, he has depth and width and can restart his body at the proper angle to block. This gives the center a better angle for leverage on the noseguard. His shoulders are almost square to the line of scrimmage, and he can get the double-under for the leverage he needs on the nose.

One thing I want to mention right now is the release by the lineman to go to the second level on the linebacker. Most of them want to get to the second level too fast. In zone blocking techniques, we want the linemen to stay on the line of scrimmage. People want to know how long you stay on the line. The answer is: forever. You cannot be in a hurry to go to the second level because the running backs are seven to nine yards deep in their alignment.

From the shotgun, the mid-zone play is not as good as from under the center. The jet sweep is good from the gun but not the mid-zone play. If you want to run a zone play from the shotgun, run the inside zone play.

I want to show you a problem in the zone play we used to have because of our scheme. The defense aligns in a 3 technique to the backside of the play and a 1 technique to the frontside. The linebackers align in a 20 technique backside and 30 technique to the playside (Diagram #10). The thing you do not want to do is take the guards off the line of scrimmage to junction the linebackers. I used to do that. Even though the playside guard releases through the B gap, there is possible leakage in that gap.

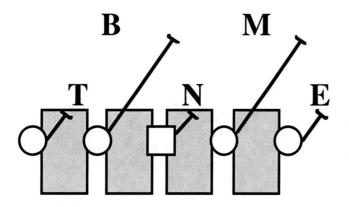

Diagram #10. Gap Leakage

Some coaches teach the guards to jam the 3 technique before he escapes to the linebacker. Alternatively, jam the nose before he escapes to the linebacker. I am saying do not do either of those techniques. I want the linemen to stay on the line of scrimmage as long as they can. Eventually, they have to leave the line because the linebackers will run away from them if they do not. However, the longer they can stay on the line, the more help they give to their partner blocking on the down defender. If they vacate the line of scrimmage after a short jam on the down defender, they open up a void or gray area inside the blocker.

The guard with the 1 technique defender has to jam the 1 technique and shuffle to the inside, keeping pressure on the 1 technique (Diagram #11). When the linebacker starts to run, the guard has to escape the line of scrimmage. However, he increases the chances of the center to make the block on the 1 technique by staying on the line of scrimmage. The center and guard want to be hip-to-hip so there is no gray area for the leakage.

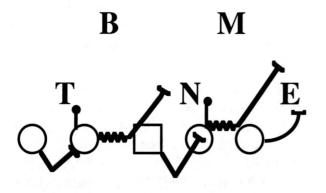

Diagram #11. Stay on the Line

The coaching point for the overlap is not to square up on the defender as you try to overlap. The offensive blocker wants to continue to work on an angle with a strong inside hand. He wants to work to free up his outside hand. As soon as the blocker squares up on the defender, the defender will play over the top of the blocker and force the ball to cut back. If the blocker can stay on the angle, it gives the back two or more steps to make a decision where to break the ball back.

If we ran the mid-zone play to the 3 technique defender with the Mike linebacker to the backside, the center would have to change his footwork (Diagram #12). The center's block is the Mike linebacker. The backside guard will overlap the center and block the 1 technique defender. The center does not take a bracer-skip to the playside because there is the threat of the 3 technique defender spiking to the inside. The center takes a lateral skip and stays on the line of scrimmage.

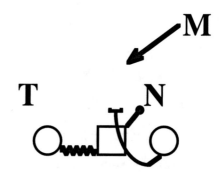

Diagram #12. Lateral Skip

We like the center's blocking assignment to be to the playside of the play. If we have one back in the backfield, we want to run the mid-zone play to the 1 technique defender. If we have two backs in the backfield, we put the center to the playside against the 3 technique and block the fullback to the backside on the Mike linebacker.

We use the square-skip against the 3-4 defense (Diagram #13). If the center has to block the 0 nose on the mid-zone play, he does a square-skip move instead of an angle reach for the noseguard. That allows him to pick up a spiking tackle stunting from the 4 technique. He takes his square step to the playside and skips with the backside foot. He is square on the line of scrimmage and can pick up a spiking tackle from the outside if necessary. The

Diagram #13. Square Skip

difference between the square and bracer skip is the depth off the line of scrimmage. The square step is slightly off the line of scrimmage. It is almost a lateral step.

If there is any coach in this room who can successfully block the pirate stunt, I want to see him. The pirate stunt in this front brings the 7 technique defensive end into an inside stick move into the B gap. The 3 technique defender runs an A gap stick. The Sam linebacker scraps the C gap, and the Mike linebacker plays over the top. Nobody knows how to block that stunt. Everyone thinks you can area block to the outside and pick up the pirate stunt. If the defense does not run the stunt, you are screwed. If they two-gap you, your play is finished. If you play a 4-3 team in a cover 2 look with no low safety, they will run the pirate stunt.

If you want to run a mid-zone play to the tight end, the offensive line has to go sideways. They have to be off the ball so they have time to convert if the front does not pirate and plays a two-gap technique. It took us some time to figure out how to block this play.

The problem we had was the reaction to the stunt going across the linemen's face (Diagram #14). The center is part of the blocking front in picking up this stunt. He moves to the playside looking to pick up a slanting defender. The center steps down the line and looks for the 3 technique coming into the

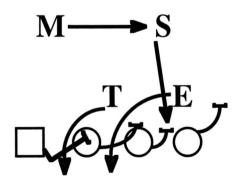

Diagram #14. Cross Face

A gap. However, on occasion the 3 technique goes behind the center as he steps into the A gap. As the playside guard, steps into the B gap, the 7 technique defender spikes and goes across his face.

The thing we did was to give the offensive linemen rules (Diagram #15). If the 7 technique spikes into the B gap, the playside guard kicks him out. If the 7 technique goes across the guard's face, the guard passes him to the center. He does not try to catch him and seal him inside. He passes him to the next blocker. That simple rule was: if the defender stayed in front of the blocker, he turned him out. If he goes underneath the blocker, he belongs to the next blocker.

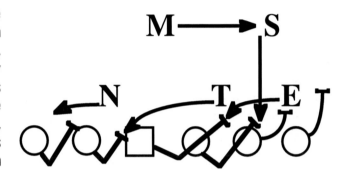

Diagram #15. Backside Guard

The backside guard has to get enough depth in his foot movement. He must be able to block his man and at the same time have enough depth to block the frontside 3 technique long sticking across the center's face.

I want to show you one more situation before we go on to the next issue. The backside tackle stepping to block the 3 technique in an overlap block can also rewind in his block (Diagram #16). The tackle takes his steps to overlap with the guard, but the 3 technique slants inside the guard. The tackle rewinds and blocks the 7 technique coming inside before he goes up to the linebacker. This helps the tight end get on the 7 technique defender.

If the guard has to block a 3 technique defender on the mid-zone play, he takes a square-skip step instead of the bracer-skip. The center has to take the bracer-skip because he is up on the line of scrimmage. The guard is off the line and does not need the depth to get into position. He takes a square step at the line. It is not a backward step. He has to take two steps to capture the leverage.

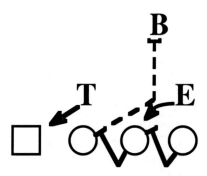

Diagram #16. Tackle Rewind

He has to step square with his outside foot and skip with the inside foot. It is a one-two movement with the feet.

The guard has to get in front of the 3 technique before he can block him. If he angles out with a reach step, the defender flattens him to the line of scrimmage. When the guard square-skips, he gets depth and width, and can leverage the defender. The sequence is to square step, skip, brace, gather, and block.

We call the finish of the block "tipping." The blocker uses the double-under move to get into the defender. At some point during the block, the blocker feels the defender start to move. When he feels that movement, he uses the momentum of the defender moving outside and tips him to the outside. He takes his inside hand, grabs the defender under the inside armpit, extends the arm, and shoves him to the outside. If he simply blocks the defender, when the ball cuts inside, the defender will fall back to the inside.

When you drill this type of work, you want the defender to fight against the tipping move. You do not want a dummy holder allowing the blocker to do what he wants. You must make the drill realistic so the blocker is prepared for what a live defender will do. The defense has to give the proper reaction to the action of the blocker or he will never learn to finish a block. Tipping the defender is simply turning the defender to the outside.

The coaching point for the tipping motion is not to let the outside leg come off the line of scrimmage and turn toward the sideline. The outside leg has to reach outside as the blocker uses his inside hand to tip the defender. If he opens his hip to the sidelines, he tips the defender into the ballcarrier.

We run some of our favorite plays to the split end side. We use this type of blocking on a stretch play going to the weakside of the formation. The tackles block is on the 5 technique defensive end. If he comes straight off the line of scrimmage and blocks the defensive end, there are two things wrong. The back arrives and the block occurs at the same time and the tackle's butt is in the hole. There is no separation between the back and the offensive lineman.

To get the separation so the back can see to make the cut, the tackle takes a quick pass set before he goes after the defensive end (Diagram #17). The tackle is not hesitating. He is taking a bracer-skip step and going like hell after the defensive end. When he does that footwork, he expands the defensive end. This is an example of a tackle to the openside of the set, letting the ball go to the inside by turning out a defender and tipping him.

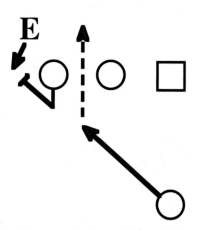

Diagram #17. Weakside Zone

I want to talk about some of the drills we use to coach technique and footwork. We use the Crowther sled to teach a flipper and drive drill. We fit the blocker into a two-man Crowther sled. He has his shoulder into the sled, pumping his feet. On the command, he brings up his inside forearm into to what we call a lazy forearm.

I want the forearm to be away from the body and lifting. This gives us more separation. The outside arm pumps with the steps taken as the player drives the sled backward. It is one blocker on a two-man sled. He wants to keep the sled straight when he drives. He takes his two-step setup and gets the sled moving. We watch to see that he stays off his toes and plants all the cleats of both feet on each step. We want the sled to stay straight as he drives it.

The next things we drill are a progression of footwork. We start out with the brace step. In the brace step, the thing you want to see is the opening of the hips. The brace foot comes back and braces the weight of the body. The opposite knee has to turn to the inside and lowers. We bend the knees in a good demeanor leg bend.

The next part of the progression is to take the second step. After the second step, you add the strike step and lock out with the double-under move. During this entire sequence, the knees remain bent. We never want the bent knees coming out of the legs.

Anthony Muñoz told me this was a good drill. The drill is simple. The blocker gets in his stance. The partner stands in front of him and puts out his hands. The drill is to see how fast a blocker can get his hands up before someone knocks them down. The blocker simply breaks his stance and fires his hands up through the extended hands of the partner. The hands of the partner are waist high.

I want to make a point that has happened to me in my coaching career. In pass protection, I love for the tackles to get wide drops to the outside. However, you cannot do that all the time. There are times when the pass rusher is too fast or the defenders run twisting moves that cause the tackle to use a vertical drop.

When you teach the vertical set, you must be demanding in the technique. The first thing I concentrate on is the outside shoulder. You cannot allow any outside turn with the outside shoulder. As you kick back at a slight angle with the outside foot, the outside shoulder has to stay parallel with the line of scrimmage.

In the footwork, we want a pigeon-toed stance with the feet. I want the knees to the inside. If the knee turns to the outside, it opens the hips in that direction. As we kick back on the toe, the shoulder does not turn outside. That technique gives the pass rusher a smaller target to hit with his hands. The only thing the blocker shows him is the point of his shoulder. If the lineman turns outside, it exposes his chest and gives the defender a tremendous amount of surface to hit.

The vertical set is a weak set. If you vertical set and turn the hips, you lose. The rusher will knock the blocker into the quarterback. In the vertical set, the shoulders must remain square to the line of scrimmage until the rusher gets past the quarterback. When that occurs, the blocker can turn and push the rusher outside. If he is in the pigeon-toed position, it is easy for him to pivot off the inside foot and ride the defender outside.

Another thing about pass protection is the angle the tackle takes, and how far he goes to the outside. If the tackle has a wide pass rusher, we coach him to take three kick-slides at a 45-degree angle to the outside. The coaching point is to make sure the shoulders stay as square as possible. Once they take the three kick-slides, they get into their pass protection routine using their hands to fight off the rusher.

If you have a long-armed tackle, a technique you can use will help. He can use a short, tight set. Instead of kicking at a 45-degree angle and intercepting the rusher, the tackle takes a flat kick to the outside and uses his outside arm to punch the rusher before he gets his second step on the ground. That allows him to take two quick steps instead of three to make the contact. He uses the length of the arm, which allows him to make the contact at a farther distance from the rusher and gives him protection against an inside move. After he makes contact, the blocker uses his pass protection techniques on the defender.

Gentlemen, I appreciate your time. I know I jumped around, and I hope I did not confuse you too much. Thank you very much.

ABOUT THE AUTHOR

Throughout Coach Jim McNally's career, he was one of the most highly regarded position coaches in the league. McNally made an immediate impact on every team when hired to coach their offensive line.

With the Bills in 2005, McNally helped second-year tackle Jason Peters develop into a starter. Peters, an undrafted free agent and former tight end at the University of Arkansas, started the final nine games of the season at right tackle. The line paved the way for Willis McGahee's career-high 1,247 yards.

With the Bills in 2004, McNally tutored an offensive line that limited opponents to 38 sacks, the lowest number allowed by a Bills team since 1998. Also with the Bills, McNally's line also paved the way for Willis McGahee to rush for 1,128 yards and 13 touchdowns in 11 starts.

Prior to retiring from the NFL with the Bills, McNally coached the offensive line for the New York Giants (1999–2003) and helped maintain offensive line success with little personnel continuity on the line during his tenure. In 2000, McNally guided an offensive line with three new players to a successful season, which culminated in the Giants' rise to the NFC championship.

Prior to joining the Giants, McNally coached the offensive line for the Carolina Panthers (1995–1998) and the Cincinnati Bengals (1980–1994). In McNally's time at Carolina, the Panthers advanced to the NFC championship game in only the team's second season of existence.

McNally's longest tenure was as the offensive line coach for the Cincinnati Bengals. In his time at Cincinnati, McNally helped establish one of the most potent rushing attacks in the league from 1986 to 1990. He coached Hall of Fame offensive tackle Anthony Muñoz, and the Bengals advanced to the Super Bowl two times during his tenure.

Before entering the NFL coaching ranks, McNally coached the offensive line at Wake Forest (1978–1979), Boston College (1975–1977), and Marshall University (1971–1974). Jim initiated his coaching career at his alma mater, University at Buffalo and coached there for six seasons (1965–1970).

NFL teams have hired McNally to be a consultant to the football staff. He spent the 2010 and 2011 football seasons with the New York Jets. He started work with the Cincinnati Bengals in 2012.

Originally from Buffalo, McNally played guard at the University at Buffalo from 1961 to 1964, and the combination of his playing career and his coaching expertise earned him a spot in the university's Hall of Fame. Now retired from coaching, Jim is nationally known for his clinics on offensive line coaching, which he conducts in the off-season.

MCNALLY AT A GLANCE

- 2012–present: Cincinnati Bengals, Offensive Consultant
- 2010–2011: New York Jets, Offensive Consultant
- 2005–present: Multiple Teams, Offensive Consultant
- 2004–2005: Buffalo Bills, Offensive Line Coach
- 1999–2003: New York Giants, Offensive Line Coach
- 1995–1998: Carolina Panthers, Offensive Line Coach
- 1980–1994: Cincinnati Bengals, Offensive Line Coach
- 1978–1979: Wake Forest University, Offensive Line Coach
- 1975–1977: Boston College, Offensive Line Coach
- 1971–1974: Marshall University, Offensive Line Coach
- 1965–1970: University of Buffalo, Offensive Line Coach

Dante Scarnecchia

PASS PROTECTION DRILLS AND TECHNIQUES

New England Patriots

Thank you very much. I really enjoy listening to all offensive line coaches lecture. Whenever I get a chance to get out and scout someone in the spring, and have the opportunity to watch practice of someone else coaching, I always try to take advantage of that. I really like to hear what other coaches have to say. More importantly, I like to hear how they say it. There are phrases you can incorporate in your teaching methods that make things a lot clearer for the players. When you hear it, it is obvious to you that they are saying something a lot better than how you have been saying it. I really try to embrace those things, so I pay close attention whenever I get the chance to hear offensive line coaches speak. This can be pretty much at all levels. There is a heck of a lot to learn out there.

What is important to me today is that you get something out of what I say, even if it is something very small. Hopefully, it will be something more than that.

I am an old guy and come from the old school. I do not use a PowerPoint® presentation like some of these younger guys. I just draw diagrams up as I go through the lecture.

What I want to show you is how we teach pass protection with the New England Patriots. I want to do that by showing you the drills we do every day. This is a great time for pro coaches because as we go into our organized team activities. It is spring practice for us. We go out in helmets, shorts, and T's. We have a practice that is about an hour and 20 minutes long. In all of that time, we only have 10 minutes of team work. That is all. We do not practice against our defense other than a 10-minute blitz period. We virtually do not work against the defense. What does that mean for me as an offensive line coach? It means I get to have about an hour and 10 minutes of individual periods throughout a practice.

We go over to our little patch of grass, and we run mostly drills. We go through run drills and pass protections drills to build a very strong foundation on how to play the game of football. All of our older veteran players have heard me coach these drills so much that it is sickening to them because we have been together for a long time. They have heard the same things over and over again. For the younger guys, though, it is especially important because we have to develop those guys into our system.

I want to start this session off by asking all of you a question. Take a look at this diagram (Diagram #1). This is not a quiz, but a poll.

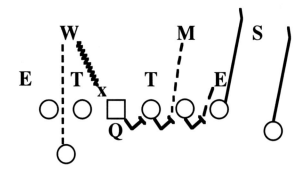

Diagram #1. Poll Question

The scenario is the quarterback is under center, and there is nothing we can do about that. The center, right guard, and tackle are going to move to the right and block that side of the line. The halfback has the Will linebacker. He has him. We are in base protection on that side. But then at the last second, the Will walks up and is on the line of scrimmage in the gap between the center and left guard. His feet are inside of the defensive tackle's feet. What are you going to do to make sure he is accounted for?

Your choices are:

a. The halfback has him.
b. Gap: The guard blocks down, and the halfback has the defensive tackle.
c. Squeeze: The guard and tackle will squeeze down, and the halfback will block the defensive end.
d. The center takes him.
e. Other.

How many of you would keep the halfback on the Will anyway?

In our informal poll, we had a few of you voting for any one of the above options. That means we have four or five different ways to try to handle this situation. We can agree we all wish this situation never happens. Guess what? It is going to happen.

My point is: it really does not matter how you handle the situation. It really doesn't. There are a lot of ways to skin a cat. What is important is: when it does happen, your players know what to do about it. All of your players have to be on the proverbial same page. What we teach may be totally different than what is taught at a lot of other places. That is absolutely okay. What is important is that our players truly understand what we want done, how we want it done, and for them to embrace it. Then, when they are given the opportunity to play, they play in the manner we want them to play. If they do that, you have a great chance to be successful.

That is what we do. We teach what we know. We teach it as best as we can and modify it as we get older and more experienced. That is what coaching is all about. I have gathered bits and pieces from everywhere and anybody I have ever listened to.

THINGS I'VE LEARNED

- Are you seeing your drills on the game tapes?
- Paint a mental picture in their minds.
- We are all connected.
- See the game through one set of eyes.

Are you seeing your drills on your game tape? Coach Tom Harper taught me this a long time ago. Tom went on to coach at several other schools, and was the defensive coordinator at Clemson University when they won the national title. He has since passed away. He was really a great football coach. He told me that if you are not seeing your drills on your game tapes, you are not doing the right drills. We make a great effort to see our drills on our game tapes.

Mike Sherman taught me the idea that you want to paint mental pictures in the minds of your players. How do you do that? You might do it with phrases. You say a phrase that means something to them so when they say it, it now makes sense to them. I have never said the phrase "Knock them out of their gap," but I heard it today, and it hit home with me. It is something I will use as I go forward. Painting mental pictures in the players' minds is the essence of coaching. That is what we are supposed to do. We have to get them to see it the way we see it. This is really important.

We want to get through to them that we are all connected in this, especially the five guys up front. Each of them has an individual and a specific job to do in order to make the play successful for everyone. If one man does not get his job done, then the entire group has failed.

We use the phase "See the game through one set of eyes" all of the time. We are trying to give them a mental picture that if all 11 players are seeing the game through one set of eyes, we have a chance to be successful. If one guy is seeing it differently than the next guy, anarchy is going to reign. It will be problematic for everyone.

Let me get into pass protection. The first thing we talk about is leverage. There are two types of leverage for us. The first is positional leverage. For us, positional leverage is putting your body between the defender and the launch point of the passer in pass protection. It is putting your body between the defender and the point of attack in the run game. Physical leverage is obvious: getting your pads under the defenders pads. For both the running and passing games, we want to have both types of leverage in everything we do.

Pass protection is a physical act. It can be difficult for some players to understand, especially the younger guys. I have heard it explained that you have to be passive to pass block. I do not believe any of that stuff. I really believe you have to be as physical in pass protection as you want them to be in the run game. We really want to hit these guys just as hard as we possibly can, with the right type of leverage and the right technique. We are going to fight for every inch of real estate we possibly can. We are going to build the wall as close to the line of scrimmage as we can.

We want our players to have fast and heavy hands. We want to punch them fast and we want to hit them with a little something. It is really important to us. We really want to hit these guys. We use that term all of the time. We say, "You have to hit them. You just can't catch them and absorb them." We are going to be proactive and hit the defense as much as we can. It is hard enough to knock them out of their rushing path.

We want to play from a position of power. As an example, if I am the right guard, I want to take on a guy from the inside out. I want my weight to be slightly inside the midline of my body. I would like my feet to be slightly wider than my shoulders, but no narrower than my armpits. I want my lower body flexed with my explosion points down low. I always want my hands up around my chest at the ready position. I have them think about forming a "W" with their hands, a few inches apart. Elbows are tight to the rib cage. When we hit these guys, we are going to hit them with everything we got as far as the upper body is concerned. We want all of the upper body power points in place.

We emphasize having the thumbs up and the fingers out. This keeps our elbows in tight. If the thumbs go down and the fingers are up, it causes the elbow to fly out. This gives the defender two handles to grab onto. You are never going to be in as strong of a position if you have your elbows pointing out. We use the butt of our hands as the primary contact point when we hit the defender. As much as we can, we want to hit them with both hands. We use the mental picture that we want to hit them with our hands from our chest to his chest. We hit what there is to hit if he dips his shoulders. We are going to hit what there is there to hit.

We want to move our feet in sequence. That might sound a little ridiculous. However, I want to try to keep my feet in constant relationship to each other. I want to keep my weight inside the midline of my body. If my weight gets outside the midline of my body when I am moving in one direction, then I will probably have to step backward before I can change directions. We constantly coach these things to them. We want to cut grass with our feet. This is a metal picture to keep our feet as close to the ground as we possibly can. This will enable us to change directions just as suddenly as the defender in front of us changes direction.

Typically, the guys we coach on the offensive side of the line are not as gifted as the guys on the defensive side. That is just the truth. We constantly tell our guys the last thing we want to try to do is to outathlete our opponents. You have no chance. We do not try to outathlete them; we play from a position of power.

We talk a lot about timing our punches. If we are in the proper position and playing from a position of power, we do not want to fire our hands until we are close enough to the defender to hit him with force. You can get into problems when getting your hands out too fast and too soon. When you hit him, you want to be close enough to hit him with a real short stroke. We put a lot of emphasis on timing the punch, and all of our drills are set up to facilitate that. All punches should come from a low to high plane. We want to do everything we can with two hands.

We want the tackles to keep the width of the pocket. We want the center and guards to keep the depth of the pocket. This is really important if you have a quarterback who is anchored in the pocket like we do.

The first drill I want to show you is the plate punch drill (Diagram #2). We line up with five cones. The first is in the center, and we have one flat down the line on each end at five yards apart. We have two more at angles at about three yards off the line.

We give each of the two linemen a 45-pound plate. They start holding the plate with their hands up against their chest in the same position we want their hands to be placed when they are ready to deliver a punch. Elbows are in tight to their rib cage. As they move laterally to the outside, they are going to move their plates just as if they are punching a defender.

We are trying to do two things here. We are trying to develop strength in their upper body so they are strong and powerful when we hit these guys. The other thing we want to do is, when we

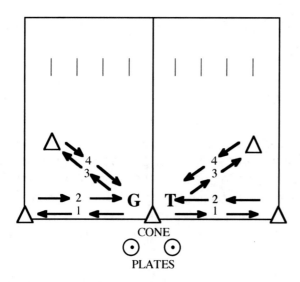

Diagram #2. Plate Punch Drill

are shuffling laterally to the outside, we are going to punch the defender by pushing off the inside foot. Each time I move my outside foot, I punch with the plate by pushing off the inside foot. When I hit the outside cone, I reverse the process and move laterally back to the inside, and hit with the plate.

While pushing off the outside foot, we are cutting grass with our feet. We want the idea of hitting the guy with as much power as we possibly can. When we move to the outside, the weight is slightly inside the midline of our body. When we go inside, the weight is still slightly inside the midline of their body. We are not tilting it back the other way because it can cause us to get off-balance, and the foot tends to fall backward. When those first two players are done, they drop the plates to the ground and the next two players pick up the plates and take their turn.

The next drill we run is the change-of-direction drill. We have the same cone setup. Now, the guys are going down the same four lines but without plates. They are moving much faster. One of the most important parts of pass blocking is changing direction because you have to react to the guy you are blocking. Every time I yell "Post," they have to change direction while following the same sequence of the four lateral lines. We use this drill to replace the mirror drill, where one big, fat lineman is trying to mirror another big, fat lineman. I do not like doing that. We have two going at the same time so we get a lot of reps, and we are going fast.

Our next drill is a four-phase set and punch drill (Diagram #3). We line up four across in two sets of two.

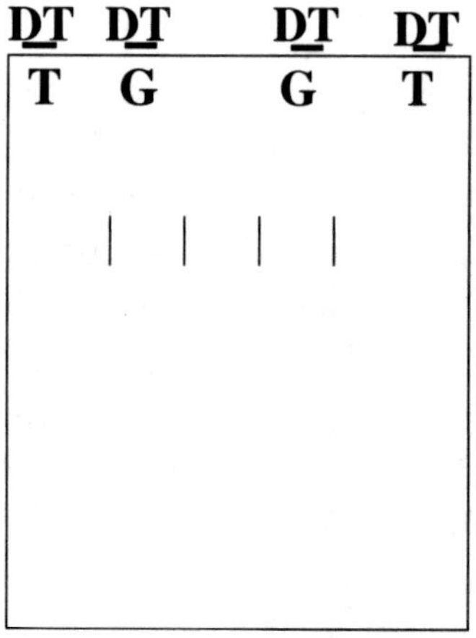

Diagram #3. Set and Punch Drill Setup

In phase one, the defensive lineman is in an inside alignment. At the snap, we are going to set that with a two-handed punch, nose-to-nose. We do that by first stepping and posting the inside foot down. We hold the post foot in place. Then, we fire our two hands from our chest to his chest, getting the power from the push from our outside foot.

The second phase is a head-up alignment. At the snap, we step and post with the inside foot, and then we set and punch them inside-out. The outside foot should not move.

In phase three, we are going to get an outside alignment in a 3 and a 5 technique alignment. We are going to step out slightly with our outside foot. The weight is still inside the midline. We are going to set or punch him off the inside foot.

In phase four, we widen the defender out. The offensive lineman takes a quick two-step, first with the outside foot and then with the inside foot. The set comes off the inside foot going out. We make sure we punch with inside-out leverage.

They end up with four phases, one right after the other, in a set and punch drill. The first phase has a nose-to-nose punch. The next three phases punch with inside-out leverage. The next guys come up and go through the same four phases.

The next drill in our progression is a replacement step drill. Our drill is set up the same way with four across. In the first phase, we have an outside 3 and 5 shade alignment. At the snap, we are going to step outside with our outside foot. If the defender goes to the inside, we are going to replace the outside foot and stab them with our hands off the outside foot going inside. We are going to meet all inside moves nose-to-nose. We stay nose-to-nose as we shuffle the defender laterally down the line of scrimmage.

In the next phase, we have the defender line up in an inside shade. We step and post with the inside foot to get nose-to-nose with the defender. If the defender goes outside, we replace the inside foot and stab the defender from the inside out. We meet the defender inside-out as he is going outside. We meet him nose-to-nose as he is going inside.

The next drill is the two-bag drill (Diagram #4).

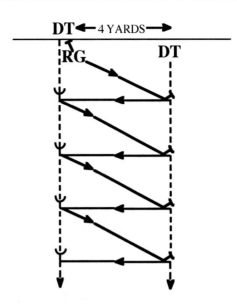

Diagram #5. Inside/Outside Drill

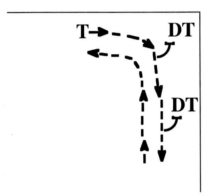

Diagram #4. Two-Bag Drill

We shuffle out at a deeper angle in this drill. It is something close to a 45-degree angle. The emphasis is to punch the defender holding a hand bag just a little bit before you get there, from our chest to his chest. We want to punch off the inside foot while going outside and the outside foot when moving in. The offensive lineman punches the first bag, shuffles, punches the second bag, and goes beyond the bags until I say "Post." Then he comes back, hitting the second bag and then the first bag. The weight is always inside the midline of the body. We want to get them moving while keeping the same learned principles.

Our next drill is an inside to outside drill, moving from an inside man to an outside man (Diagram #5).

Here, we are working with the right guard. At the snap, he is going to step with his left foot and set and punch the defensive tackle in front of him, nose-to-nose. Then, he shuffles at an angle to take on the defensive tackle, who is set up to his outside. He will set him up inside-out. Both defenders are about four yards apart and maintain a parallel relationship to each other as they progress up the field. Our guard then shuffles back to his inside defender, but he has to shuffle flat, parallel to the line of scrimmage. As the right guard, if he shuffles back at an angle, he will shuffle into our quarterback, so he has to stay flat.

Another variation of the two-bag drill is the three-bag drill (Diagram #6).

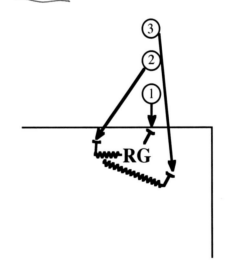

Diagram #6. Three-Bag Drill

The first defensive man with a bag is lined up outside of the offensive lineman. At the snap, the offensive player takes the outside rusher on, inside-out. After he sets on the first man, he will shuffle laterally to take on the second man. The second defensive man runs at him at an angle that starts outside the shoulder, and the point of contact is the inside shoulder of the offensive pass blocker. The offensive lineman takes him on nose-to-nose. The offensive lineman sets and disposes of the second guy and shuffles at an angle to take on the third rusher. The third defender takes an outside rushing path, and our offensive lineman takes him on, inside-out.

A variation we use on this drill is to have the third rusher as a bull rusher that tries to run over the blocker. As the blocker delivers the blow, he has to widen his feet in order to break the defender down. He uses one foot as a break to stop the momentum of the bull rusher. We can also align the defender from off the shoulder to the next gap or wider.

What are we trying to do here? We want to get them to move and change direction. We want them to play from a position of power. We want to cut grass with our feet. We want them to strike from our chest to his chest. These are all the things we learned in the earlier drills, but now on a larger scale with more movement as we go. Now, we want them to see more than one defender. These are the natural progressions of what we ultimately want to accomplish and see on film.

Next, we move on to our line stunt drills. I sit over in my own little world with these big, fat offensive linemen. The hardest thing to do is to try to get offensive linemen to emulate defensive players running line stunts. They are terrible at it. I got frustrated with it, so I developed another two-bag drill that would simulate a two-man stunt (Diagram #7).

We want the defensive tackle to roar off the right guard's outside shoulder on a vertical line just as fast as he can go. The bag guy who is staggered off the line is to simulate a defensive end coming around on a tackle-end stunt. We have him staggered because our people holding the bags could never get there in time to give us a good look. If we lined him up on the line like a true defensive

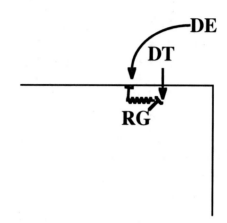

Diagram #7. Two-Bag Tackle-End Stunt Drill

end, he would never get there. We actually want it to happen faster than what it would normally happen.

The idea is we want the blocker to see more than one guy. We want him to see through the first guy. We are going to smash the drive guy on the tackle-end stunt from the inside out, but we also want to get our eyes ahead and see two defenders. He takes a lateral shuffle down the line to the defensive end and takes him on nose-to-nose because he is coming to our inside. That is what we teach. That is what we believe in.

We do the same concept with the tackle. We simulate a defensive end and a defensive tackle stunt (Diagram #8).

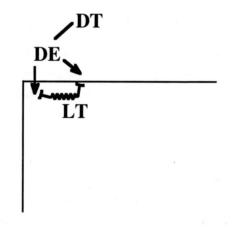

Diagram #8. End-Tackle Stunt With Left Tackle

The tackle meets the defensive end going across his face, nose-to-nose. He meets the tackle going around the defensive end from the inside out.

Let me show you one last thing that we do. I really like this because I think it puts everything together. This is a triangle drill (Diagram #9).

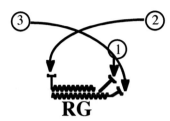

Diagram #9. Triangle Stunt Drill

The first defensive lineman goes upfield as fast as he can go. We meet him inside-out. We want to come flat down the line of scrimmage to meet the second defender nose-to-nose. We bring the third defender into it as if they were running a three-man stunt. We meet him inside-out.

What are we trying to do? We want them to work the techniques we teach. We want them firing off with the proper foot. We keep our weight on the inside of our midline. We get our eyes ahead to see through the first guy to the second guy. I think this is a good way to simulate line stunts the best way we can because they are hard to simulate.

Here is one thing we do that is probably different than what most other teams do. When we have 1-on-1 pass blocking drills against the number-one defense, we line up our entire front five. We do this to give the spacing cues we need, and it also helps keep the defensive rusher in their proper pass rushing lanes. They are not able to take exaggerated pass lanes to get to the quarterback that are not realistic in game situations. The only two live guys are the rusher and the pass blocker responsible for him. The others get in their stance and take their first step at the snap.

I want you to know that I have a tremendous amount of respect for coaches out there, including defensive line coaches. Every week, they really work hard to present as many problems as they can for all of us offensive line coaches. It is a huge challenge every week.

I really believe you have to have a strong foundation of techniques that will allow you to get the defenders covered up. Our league is driven by the man taking the ball from center. Protecting that guy at all costs is the essence of everything we do. If that guy is on his back, we have no chance. There is not one coach on our staff, including our head coach, who believes we have the answers to everything. We just have ways of doing things that we feel really strongly about. We feel if our players can embrace those things and do them as well as they can do them, we have a chance to be successful. All we care about is having a chance to be successful.

I really appreciate your time today. This has been a great pleasure for me. Thank you very much.

ABOUT THE AUTHOR

Dante Scarnecchia is a 40-year coaching veteran, who is enjoying his 28th season as an NFL assistant. He has the longest coaching tenure in Patriots' history, now entering his 26th season on the Patriots sidelines. Since joining the Patriots in 1982, he has spent all but two seasons (1989–1990) in Foxborough.

Scarnecchia has the distinction of being the only coach in franchise history to be a member of all six of its Super Bowl teams. He has been on the Patriots coaching staff during 13 of the franchise's 16 playoff appearances and has coached in 30 of the 34 playoff games in team history.

For the 11th consecutive season, Scarnecchia's primary responsibility will be the offensive line, a position he has coached for 24 of his 40 seasons in the profession. Bill Belichick named Scarnecchia the Patriots' assistant head coach/offensive line coach on February 1, 2000.

In the 2011 season, the offensive line helped produce the best rushing season in more than 20 years for the Patriots. New England averaged 4.4 yards per carry and totaled 2,278 yards and 21 rushing touchdowns. The offensive line also helped to consistently sustain drives, as the Patriots led the league in drives of 10 plays or longer (38) and in rushing first downs (145).

In 2007, Scarnecchia was named SI.com's NFL Assistant Coach of the Year. Anchored by an offensive line that sent three players to the Pro Bowl (center Dan Koppen, tackle Matt Light, and guard Logan Mankins), the Patriots offense broke several NFL records, including points scored and touchdowns scored. The offensive line powered a Patriots rushing attack that posted the franchise's highest average yards per rush in 22 years (4.10). The offensive line also allowed just 21 sacks in the regular season, the lowest total for the franchise since the NFL adopted a 16-game schedule. Protected by the line, NFL MVP Tom Brady broke the NFL record for touchdown passes in a season (50) and led the league in both passing yards (4,806, also a franchise record) and passer rating (117.2, also a franchise record).

New England's protection up front was a significant contributor to the team's three Super Bowl winning seasons. In 2004, the line opened holes for running back Corey Dillon to set a single-season franchise record with 1,635 rushing yards and led the NFL with 109.0 yards per game. In 2003, the offensive line did not allow a sack in any of the team's three postseason games despite 126 pass attempts. In 2001, Scarnecchia worked with a unit that featured three new starters, but still produced a powerful rushing attack and a balanced passing attack on the way to the franchise's first Super Bowl victory.

Prior to becoming offensive line coach, Scarnecchia coached the Patriots special teams units for two seasons (1997–1998).

Scarnecchia originally joined the Patriots and made his NFL coaching debut in 1982 as a member of Ron Meyer's staff. He coached the tight ends and special teams for the Patriots for seven seasons (1982–1988) before moving on to Indianapolis with Meyer in 1989. He rejoined the Patriots in 1991 after spending two seasons (1989–1990) as the Colts' offensive line coach. From 1991 to 1992, he coached the tight ends and special teams on Dick MacPherson's staff. On November 4, 1992, MacPherson fell ill and appointed Scarnecchia to serve as the team's spokesman in his absence. Scarnecchia fulfilled the obligation for seven of the Patriots' final eight games and held the responsibilities of the head coach for both of the Patriots' victories that season.

In 1993, he was the only Patriots assistant retained from the previous staff. He was appointed special assistant from 1993 to 1994, which was redefined as defensive assistant from 1995 to 1996. During that time, he assisted defensive coordinator Al Groh with the development of the team's linebacking corps.

His coaching career began in 1970 as the offensive line coach at California Western University. He moved to Iowa State University in 1973, where he served as the assistant offensive line and assistant defensive backfield coach. He spent the 1975 and 1976 campaigns at Southern Methodist University, before becoming the University of the Pacific's offensive line coach and recruiting coordinator from 1977 through 1978. In 1979, Scarnecchia coached at Northern Arizona University and then accepted an opportunity to return to Meyer's staff at SMU as the offensive line coach in 1980 and 1981. In 1982, Meyer was hired as the head coach of the New England Patriots, and Scarnecchia was among a number of the SMU assistants who joined Meyer's staff in New England.

Mike Solari

DEVELOPING THE RUN GAME WITH FUNDAMENTALS AND DRILLS

San Francisco 49ers

The first thing is this question: Who has it better than us? Who has it better than us? That is right; nobody has it better than us! We are doing what we love.

Men, what color is this napkin? Louder! What color is this napkin? Bring some passion and energy; let me hear it. What color is this napkin? (White!) What do cows drink? (Milk.) No, water!

It is very important that we all stay together here. What is important here is this: Are you hearing, or are you listening? We are going to ask you to listen during this whole presentation.

This clinic is awesome! I am glad I was able to get here early this morning so I could hear the speakers. It was outstanding.

Just like we tell our offensive linemen, do you know the following:
- People hear 50 percent of what is said.
- They understand 50 percent of what they hear.
- They believe 50 percent of what they understand.
- They remember 50 percent of what they believe.
- This means they remember six percent of what was originally said.

I am asking you to take notes. That is the key thing we are going to ask you to do. I am not going to get into it very deep today, but this is something we believe in at the San Francisco 49ers.

SHIFTS AND MOTIONS

We use shifts and motions to give us the advantage by gaining leverage, disguising formations and creating match ups. Multiple shifts and motions cause confusion and make the defense practice multiple looks; ultimately, they are forced into vanilla fronts.

We shift and motion on the command by the quarterback. We must be set more quickly and precisely in sequence to give us an advantage in breaking down the containment or force element.

We really believe this. We have a great group of coaches, and Jim Harbaugh is an outstanding head coach. He makes it easy for the assistant coaches to do what it is we like to do, and that is to coach. Jim takes care of the players. He is awesome with discipline. We have great coaches who bring energy and love to teach. It takes good coaches to be successful, but it also takes good players.

There is no better asset we have to try to get an advantage on the offensive side of the ball than shifts and motions. Not all of us have that great quarterback. I am talking to the men in this room. Study how you can outleverage the contain player. How can you motion and get the force element on the other side where you are running the ball? We take a lot of time, as individuals and as a group, studying how we can gain an advantage for next year with shifts and motions.

Let me give you a tip with shifts and motions. Your shifts have got to be dynamic. Offensive line, we have to get set. The motions have to be specific. Offensive line coaches, you may have to step up if you have a young receiver coach who does not have the exact understanding of what you want, in the sense of the inside leg of the tackle, the outside leg of the guard, or the outside leg of the tackle. It is specific as to where that snap point needs to be in order to make a particular play successful.

Everybody believes it is our job to get our group to be the best! We do that with:
- Fundamentals
- Explosiveness
- Techniques
- Finish

We have to teach fundamentals and techniques. That is our job.

We want to be explosive. I can remember vividly talking with Bill Walsh, when we were with the 49ers together, about beating the opponent to the punch. It is like being a boxer and beating them to the punch. Everybody is big and strong. If you keep punching them, if you keep hitting them in the mouth, you will wear them down.

The next thing you have to do is finish. There is a tremendous range of accomplishment when you talk about finish. You have to push it, and you have to stress it. Do not be denied with what you want.

I stole this chart from Brad Seely, our special teams coach. I am telling you what; he is good. I stole it because it is so, so true. It is all about attitude.

Attitude
Determines
Preparation
Determines
Performance
Determines
Success!

I am talking about coaches, also. Bring some energy into your room. There is no doubt about it that is what it is all about.

Our job as an offensive line coach is to create synergy.

Synergy: Working together, combined action of operation, that the total effect is greater than the sum of the individual effects.

We have to get our five guys to work as one. Nobody said it better than what I heard from Dante Scarnecchia earlier today. You want them to see it through one set of eyes. We want to get them to work better together than if we were to get them to work individually. I truly believe it is one heartbeat for the offensive line.

TOOLS OF THE OFFENSIVE LINE

- Splits
- Alignment
- Snap count

Our line splits are 18 inches. There is absolutely an accordion effect about it in the sense of inside runs, draws, and screens. On screens, we want a little bit bigger splits. Why? Because we have to snap the ball, get rid of the guys, and get out on the alley or the flat in order to block our defenders. If we are in a goal line situation, we want six-inch splits. If we are in a short yardage situation, we want 12-inch splits.

If you are in goal line versus a 6-2 defense where the defensive tackles are in the gaps and they are shading on the center, do you see it? There, I do not want the guards to have a six-inch split. In that situation, I want it a little bit tighter, like three-inch splits.

Say we are going up against a goal line 5-3 defense. Do you see it? There is a nose tackle lined up on the center, and he is going to hit him in the mouth. You also have to deal with the 3 techniques. They are lined up on the outside shoulders of the guards. That week, I would want a little bit bigger split. The splits will adjust. You have to do what is best for you, but you want to coach splits. This is an offensive tool for the offensive line.

As far as alignment goes, we want our down hand on the toes of the center. When we watch practice or game film, the down linemen better have their hand where it is supposed to be. This is part of a tool we want to take advantage of. When we get short yardage or goal line, we tell them to take "all of the ball." I coach taking all of the ball every day in those situations, and sometimes we still will not take all of the ball. You have to coach it.

Depending on the level of your players, you may have to really coach it. It is a tremendous advantage on goal line and short yardage because you cannot have any penetration. None. Nada! So you, therefore, want to take all of the ball. We will not have penetration, and we will have a surge on the line of scrimmage. You have to coach it. It is a very, very important coaching point.

Our guard's inside toe is at the heel of the center. NFL rules require us to break the belt buckle of the center's alignment. Our tackle's inside toe has to be aligned on the guard's inside toe. It is a common error that our tackle lines his inside toe with the outside toe of the guard. It has to be the inside toe so the alignment is proper.

I am not sure where everybody here is on a silent count. When our quarterback is under center, I want our guys to be back just a little bit. Not everybody believes that, and that is okay. We want the guard's hand to split the foot of the center. Why? So the tackles can see down the line of scrimmage to get the silent count cue from the center's helmet.

We want to stress these fundamentals in the run game.

Stance: Balanced. If I have a shorter guy, I am going to go toe to instep. If I have a longer guy, I am going toe to heel. I want their feet shoulder-width apart.

Initial Quickness: Explosive. Getting out of your stance is the most important thing. We have got to beat the defense to the punch. We know the cadence. We have to show quick explosive movement out of our stance.

Footwork: Trace. On every play, we are going to tell the offensive linemen where their aiming point is, what his footwork is, what his inside hand is doing, and what his outside hand is doing. On every play, the offensive lineman will know exactly what we want from him in order to execute.

Strike: Leverage. The strike has to be with leverage. We are going to hit you in the mouth. We are going to come off the ball.

Fractional Time: Accelerate the feet on contact. Once you strike and roll your feet, you have to accelerate your feet. It is very important. We want to speed up the process.

Base: All the cleats in the ground. I am coaching the second step. *I am coaching the second step!* The second step has got to get down. The second step never, ever, splits the midline. The second step has to get vertical. Not lateral, vertical. I coach my tail off on the second step. Do not go laterally because you are not coming off the ball. We are going to come off the ball.

I like all of the cleats in the ground. When we go out to look for offensive linemen, we are looking for guys who can play on their feet. The great ones play with all of their cleats in the ground. You do not have great ones yet. You are working with them.

Ankle flexibility is important in line play in order to get maximum power. This may be something you want to work on. If you are flexible at the ankles, knees, and hips, you are going to be explosive. Why? Because all of the joints are ready to fire. We have to coach them to be more explosive. We have to coach them to improve their initial quickness and to come out of their stance. That is our job as coaches. You isolate it, and you drill it.

If you take anything from my talk today, take this: I learned this from Bill Walsh. He said, "Mike, if you want something, isolate it, and drill it." Wow! What a statement. Dante Scarnecchia said, "Are you seeing it on the game tape?" Are you seeing it on Friday or Saturday night? If you want your guys to cut on the backside, you drill it. Be specific with them, and drill it. You coach it. The best runs in the NFL are when the backside A and B gaps are cut off. Those are the 20-, 30-, and 40-yard plus runs. The best technique you can coach on this, without a doubt, is to cut them. Nobody coaches the cut block, I mean *nobody* teaches the cut block better than Bobb McKittrick of the San Francisco 49ers.

You guys are too young to remember this. Back in the day, Howie Long, the player, went after Bobb McKittrick, the coach, because he was getting his butt cut. He went after Bobb, and all of the offensive linemen rallied around Bobb. Defensive linemen do not want to get cut. The guy who stole it from Bobb was Mike Shanahan, who took it to Denver. It worked out pretty good there.

Finish: Hands on.

Following are the fundamentals we want to stress in the pass game.

Stance: Balanced three-point or two-point. We are going out of a three-point stance except for third down. On third down, the tackles are up. In the two-minute offense, everybody is up.

Set: Initial sequence. We coach the center on three points. We want the off hand to come up, the ball to be snapped, and the right foot to all work in coordination at the same time. If I am a right-handed snapper, I want the right foot, ball, and left hand up in a hitting position. How quickly can he get into that position?

If the nose tackle is off the center, I am not so worried about the off hand. The off hand gives me separation. This is a key coaching point. When the center snaps the ball, do not have him cross with his off hand. It is straight ahead. When do I not set the third point with the right foot? When the shade is on his left shoulder. My three points are left foot, ball, and left hand.

I am not worried about the off hand if the defender is not tight. It just buys separation until I can get my second hand up. If he is off, I am going to double-hand punch him.

In passing situations, we are going to have the tackles narrow their base. Tackles also want a narrow base on screens and draws. It has to look exactly the same.

The San Francisco 49ers are going to have the center point to where we are going. You got that? The 49ers point to where they are going in the pass game so they know who they got. Guess what? We point in the run game, too.

Just to keep it consistent, we cannot just point in the pass game without pointing in the run game. Some defensive coaches like to play games when you start to point so you have to be consistent with pointing on runs so you do not give your play away.

Eyes: Inside armpit. I have always coached, when you set, you eyeball the inside number. When you pass set, you want to be on the inside number. About game four of last year, I told the tackles to eyeball the inside armpit. I like it a lot.

When the tackle sets, I want him looking at the inside armpit. Too many guys are looking at the helmet. We have got to break them of that habit. You have to train their eyes. We are training their eyes at our level. They have to be able to see through who they are blocking, for the most dangerous man.

Hands Up: Thumbs up. When we punch, thumbs are up. I love using the cuffs. It teaches them to keep their hands in and thumbs up. We want to use the tools available to us to help them and to coach them. That is what we do. It is an ongoing process.

Base: Balanced.

Punch: Inside number. We utilize the double-hand punch, but we emphasize the importance of the inside hand. We want them to punch the inside edge of the inside number with the inside hand. I want the second hand on the outside number. We want to hit with both hands, but there can be a point where the outside numbers are too far away. If I were to punch it, my weight will have to transfer to my outside foot. I do not want that. The weight stays on the inside leg. I am going to be patient and may have to have a one-two punch. If he turns into me, it is two hands without a doubt.

If the defensive end is in a speed rush upfield, the tackle is going to punch with his inside hand. He is not going to commit the outside hand. This is the only time we will tell the tackle to be ready to clasp the outside shoulder with his outside hand. If the end turns in, the outside hand is on the outside number right away. The outside foot has to be ready to move.

Kick Slide: Drag the inside toe. If I am the right guard or right tackle, when I work to my outside, I want to drag the inside toe on the ground. We do it this way because it keeps the weight on the inside leg.

Another coaching point on the finish is this: I truly believe if you watch us on film, you will see this. When the ball is thrown, you will see our lineman cover. In practice, they have to cover for 10 yards. If we are in a walk-through, you will see us cover for 10 yards. But it's a walk-through. *Men, it is 10 yards!* The offensive linemen can tell when the defensive rushers separate. They go cover. It is also part of conditioning. When they cover, they cover to the ball. They have got to find the ball.

If there is ever a turnover, you are going to diminish the return. You should teach your young offensive linemen: the first guy makes the tackle; the second guy strips the ball. Coach it. You will get one. It might not be every year; it might be the third year. Most defenders are not used to carrying the ball. They will give up one, if you coach it.

Let me move on to the two-man Crowther sled progression on my film. This is a six-point progression. We work with one man at a time. (Film)

Pendulum Swing: We want them in a good two-point stance and in a good hitting position one foot away from the sled pad. Their toes are pointed straight ahead with ankles, knees, and hips flexed. They straddle the outside of one of the pads on the two-man sled so their inside shoulder is lined up with the pad. Their hands are hanging down and relaxed. It is a pendulum swing, where they learn to hit it with the back part of their hand. They swing both hands upward. There is no windup. The back of the inside hand will hit the pad while the outside hand swings above shoulder height.

Forming Triangle: They start from the same position. Now, once they strike the pad with the backside of their hand, they bring their forearm up and in front of them to form the bottom part of a triangle at shoulder height. They still want to throw their off hand because it will help them bring their hips. It will give them the feel, when they are coming off the ball, of rolling their hips. We do not want them to wind up with the hitting hand. We do not want them to strike the pad, at this point, with their forearm or shoulder. The idea here is to develop initial explosive movement.

Some of you may say, "We do not do that anymore. We use our hands." I am telling you, when we come off the ball on combination blocks, we use a shoulder roll. Why? If you want a guy to strike, their pads have got to be down. *If you want a guy to strike, their pads have got to be down. Down!* If you are using your hands to strike, your shoulders are going to be too high. If you are playing against big people on defense, your pads have got to be down.

Rolling the Hips: You are not going to knock anybody off the ball if you do not roll your hips. *You are not knocking anybody off the ball unless you roll your hips!* You better be able to roll your hips.

They now start from their knees, still one yard away from the pad. You want them to have their toes curled and in the ground behind them. They want to roll their hips, and strike with their shoulder. They still swing the off hand like a pendulum so they stay square. The player will be flat on his stomach after they strike and the sled moves. If they are doing it right, they are going to roll on their lower abdomen. Do not let them put their hand out to catch themselves. That means they are not throwing the off hand.

Stance, Rolling the Hips: They are starting in their stance. They want to roll their hips and strike the pad with their forearm and shoulder. Use the same pendulum swing with the off hand to emphasize rolling the hips. The finish is the same as before, with a roll on their lower abdomen. The Crowther sled is a great machine. It is a great tool. If you do not have enough time to use it on the field, throw it in your weight room. Teach your strength coach how to hit it properly and have him work with your young kids. Whatever you have got to do, implement it. You can figure out a way.

One Step, Rolling the Hips: They take one step and then roll their hips. Always step forward. Start with a left step, roll the hips, and strike with the right forearm and shoulder. Throw the off hand. The finish will be the same. Switch sides and also, practice power, stepping with the inside foot and striking with the inside shoulder.

One Step, Rolling the Hips, and Driving the Feet: We add driving their feet. They take one step, roll their hips, strike with the arm and shoulder, and then drive their feet. Next, they are going to pump with the off arm, keeping the elbow in tight. That is a good coaching point. Make sure they pump the off arm. We want to see quick feet. We are looking at fractional time, the strike, and the acceleration of the feet. How much weight they put on their feet will be determined by the condition of the surface. If the grass is wet, less weight. If they are on the turf, they will want to put a little more weight on their feet.

Arm Roll, Second-Level Strike: They want to come off on a combination block. After they drive the sled for a few yards, they come off and accelerate to block the next man holding a hand pad. We are going to coach a double-under technique on the second level.

I truly believe in pads down, striking with your shoulders, coming off the ball, and hit them in the mouth mentality. You have to play the game physically. You run the ball to win the game. You throw the ball to win championships. You have to be able to pass to win the championship. You are going to face a pretty salty defense in the championship game. You will have to be able to pass it then. To win the Super Bowl, you have to be able to pass the ball. It is a fact.

Another drill we like to use on the Crowther sled is the two-hand punch. We go one at a time again. This is not the double-under, but you are getting the same thing. They are coming out of their stance with tight hands and shooting their hands with the thumbs up. They are going to hit the Crowther with their hands, roll their hips, and move their feet.

We do not want a lot of weight on the Crowther because we want them to get the feeling of rolling their hips and getting their feet in the ground. We want to take note of hand placement, rolling the hips, moving their feet, and all the cleats in the ground.

Let me go over a simple play with you. It is a 60/70 power. It is a staple play in any offense. This is a gap scheme play.

RULES

- We want to identify the front.
- Block the inside gap first.
- Going to people on paper, but responsible for your gap first.
- Maximize numbers. Double-team whenever you can!
- If someone shows on your track, he gets hit and blocked.
- Not going to complicate a physical, explosive, violent play once the ball is snapped. Power! Leverage is the winning edge! Feet! Acceleration through targets!

We are going to get an edge. How do you do it? Maybe you go Zebra with three receivers, one tight end, and one back. We are reducing. The tight end is on a single. If the defense is in a wide 9 technique, we are going to run a power play.

We might go with two tight ends and two backs. If we get a head-up technique, we are going to run power from that formation. We are going to get that edge.

We go big wing with a tight end, a wing, and then another wing. In case you are not getting it, we are going to get an edge, and we are going to run power. We put seven linemen in the game; we do not care. We are going to get an edge. We figure out how we are going to do that from our study of the opponent.

We are not going to complicate this play; we are coming off the ball.

MUSTS

- *Grab grass:* The post man has to grab grass with his inside foot. If the inside foot goes back, he cannot roll his hips. The first step is short, but it has to grab grass. It is like a repost, but it positions us to roll our hips. You have got to roll your hips on power! We have got to knock their fannies off the ball.
- *Gain ground*
- *Low to high*

It is a pure attitude power play. This is an attitude play for the 49ers. We are going to come off the ball. It is a nasty, explosive, violent, simple play. It is gap scheme.

GAP PRINCIPLES

- No penetration
  ✓ No penetration
  ✓ No penetration
- Never get caught backside
- Puller: Tight to the double-team
- Kickout block: Inside-out
- RB: Read the alphabet A to D

Take a simple play, and coach it simple. This is the 60/70 power versus a 25 front (Diagram #1).

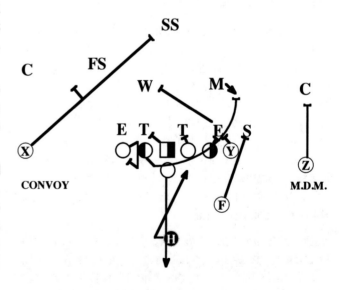

Diagram #1. 60/70 Power vs. 25 Front

RB: Shoulders square. A, B, C, D gaps. We are taking it inside. We are running off the deuce.

QB: Give him room; no penetration!

Trapper: Inside-out

Wrapper: Strike a match off the double-team. Come up nice and tight and square. You want the inside number of the linebacker. You want him to strike the inside number of the linebacker coming off the double-team.

WR: Block the force.

RT: Grab grass with the inside foot. The outside knee is driving through the crotch.

TE: Driver, The outside guy steps with his inside foot. The most important thing is to get his inside shoulder on the outside shoulder of the defender. The second step has to get down quickly because that is where the force is coming from. If he takes too big of a step, he has no base, and he will not get the movement we need. If you have a wide 5 technique, the tight end will step up and in. Other than that, the inside shoulder is on the outside shoulder.

RG: Grab grass with the inside foot. He cannot step back. The aiming point is the frontside shoulder. Inside hand is on the sternum on all down blocks. *On all down blocks.* The outside hand is the clasp hand and strikes the rib cage with the thumbs up. Drive the defender flat down the line. On the strike, work the helmet up the field, vertically.

We scout our opponent to see how they handle a down block. Do they punch and lock arms and fight across it? Do they try to rip through it? Whatever they do, your scout team has to work it that way for that week's practice. You have to be that detailed. You have to be a master offensive line coach and know how they play the down block. How do they play the double-team? Do they get low and try to split it, or do they take a knee? However they do it, your scout team has to play it that way for the entire week of practice.

It is our job to coach up the scout team. It is our job as an offensive line coach to teach a shield holder how to hold a shield properly. If you want your linemen to come of the ball low, look at the drill on film. Is your bag holder holding the bag down low? We want them to work at an angle they are going to see in a game situation. Isolate it; drill it. What you want, you coach.

C: Block back. He is still on the frontside shoulder. The wider the tackle is, the flatter his step. If he is tight, he has got to get his foot down quickly. The key is the second step. Once he makes contact, drive his feet.

BST: Jab and pick. Secure the B gap. The backside tackle has to step and be ready to double clutch to the inside for a zone blitz. On a zone blitz, he will have to come down and drag the 3 technique out. Other than that, he takes an inside step and gets his shoulder, not hand, on the 3 technique before he comes back out.

If we get a 45 front, we are going to double the 3 technique (Diagram #2). You have to make a line call to let the tight end know he is on a single.

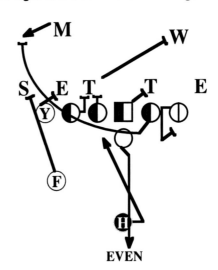

Diagram #2. 60/70 Power vs. 45 Front

LG: Step with the inside foot, and drive the second knee through the crotch. The post man should never, ever step with the outside foot. Always step with the inside foot.

LT: Step with the inside foot, and get the inside shoulder on the outside shoulder of the defender. Deuce with LG on the Will linebacker.

TE: Down block rule. Inside footwork to grab grass. Aiming point is the frontside shoulder of the defensive end. Frontside hand on the sternum, outside hand is the clasp hand. Once he strikes, drive him.

RG: Pulling and lighting a match off the rear end of the tight end.

We can run it against a 34 front (Diagram #3). Here, we are going to paint a picket fence.

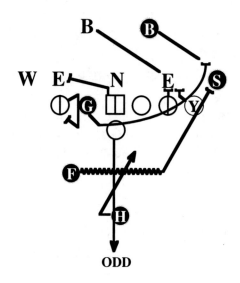

Diagram #3. 60/70 Power vs. 34 Front

C: Step with the backside foot like he is making a back block. He has the run-through by the buck linebacker. If the defensive end spikes, he has him. If the end goes outside, the tackle will collect him, and he now has the outside shoulder of the backside Will linebacker folding over the top.

RT: Double-team with the tight end.

Let me give you one more look. This is against a 57 Bear front (Diagram #4). You cannot use this line scheme every week because they will start to run twists, but if you have a 3 technique who does not chase the pulling guard, this is a better blocking scheme. If he is a slow guy, the left tackle can cut him, and you still have the deuce man seal. Do not expect the tackle to cut him if you did not drill it. It is not fair. You have to drill it if you expect it to get done.

You do not want a negative yardage play. You should not have a negative yardage play on such a simple play. It is gap blocking. It is an attitude play where you are coming off the ball and you are going to hit them in the mouth.

You are going to run it again, and again, and again. In the first quarter, you are going to make three yards. What? Yes, three yards. In the second

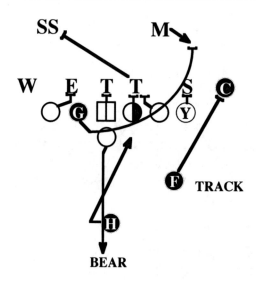

Diagram #4. 60/70 Power vs. 57 Bear Front

quarter, you are going to make four maybe five yards. Third quarter, you might get six or seven. In the fourth quarter, you are going to get double-digit runs. You are going to pound their butts.

In the NFL, there are no holes in the first half; there are literally creases. If you start banging them, banging them, and banging them, all of a sudden those creases start to become holes. You have to bring your will.

Men, I am going to go to some film because film tells the story. (Film)

This is a great drill we stole from Howard Mudd of the Philadelphia Eagles. If you want the guard to turn up and be square after he strikes the match on the double-team, run this drill (Diagram #5).

Diagram #5. Softball Drill

Place two bags or garbage cans standing up on the ground to represent the double-team. Place a softball on the ground just a few feet past the bags. Have the guard, or whoever you are coaching, pull and strike a match on the bags, and then turn up and pick up the softball with his inside hand. Make him touch the bags with his hip. You want to see the bag waver. That is a great drill to get them to turn up and get square in the hole. Great drill! Your linemen can even do it in the summer when you are not even there.

Men, here is a complementary run. We call it cab/storm (Diagram #6). This is from my Kansas City days. We want to find out how we can out leverage the defense. If they play wide, we are running power. If they play tight, we are running cab/storm. We are pulling and coming around the corner. It is as simple as down, down for the tight end and the wing. The tackle is pulling and kicking out the force. He is kicking out the widest. Down, down, get around. The fullback is searching to the inside, looking for the alley player. The backside is blocking wide zone. On the backside get them on the ground, cut them.

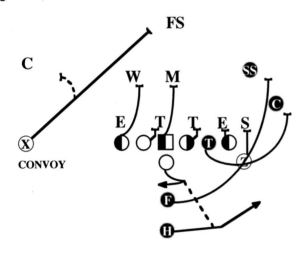

Diagram #6. Cab/Storm

On all perimeter runs, the lineman pulling around has to aim for the outside number. The reason why you want the outside number is because the defensive coach is telling his players not to give up the outside number. When you are running a track to the outside number, the defender is going to go outside that track. You will hit the inside number. A common mistake is to idle down. You cannot let them do it. They need to run through the man. You want to get a double-under, lift him up, and run your feet. Run your feet. Do not jackknife your legs, or you will trip up the running back. If you track the outside number, it will help you increase the running lane for the back. The back knows we are tracking the outside number. He will run to the outside, and then he will cut back inside off the block.

They cannot stop both plays, the power and the cab/storm. Complement your power play with the formation. Have a hit-them-in-the-mouth play and then an outside play from the same formation. It does not really matter what the formation is. Have it look the same. Then, have a lead play. Add a weakside play. Then, you really got them. You got them!

Thank you very much.

ABOUT THE AUTHOR

Mike Solari rejoined the 49ers in 2010 as the team's offensive line coach, after having previously served as the tight ends/assistant offensive line coach for San Francisco from 1992 to 1996 under legendary coach Bobb McKittrick. In his role, Solari works closely with offensive line coach Tim Drevno.

Under the direction of Solari and Drevno, the 49ers offensive line showed stability and growth in 2011. Joe Staley (tackle), Mike Iupati (guard), Jonathan Goodwin (center), and Anthony Davis (tackle) started every game that season, while Adam Snyder (guard) started the final 13 regular season games and both postseason contests. Staley was named second-team All-Pro and was selected to his first Pro Bowl as a starter, while Iupati and Goodwin were named Pro Bowl alternates.

The offensive line led the way for running back Frank Gore as he became the franchise's all-time leading rusher, surpassing Hall of Famer Joe "The Jet" Perry. Gore, who was also selected to the Pro Bowl, set the franchise record rushing for over 100 yards in five consecutive games. He finished the season ranked sixth in the NFL with 1,211 rushing yards in 2011. The offense finished the season with the league's eighth-best run game.

In 2010, Solari relied on his extensive experience as he helped shuffle an offensive line that was plagued by injury, while also integrating first-round draft picks Anthony Davis and Mike Iupati into the starting lineup. After a season-ending injury to starting center Eric Heitmann in training camp,

Solari was able to quickly find a replacement in David Baas, who hadn't started a game at center since college. Baas went on to start all 16 games for the 49ers and earned the coveted Bobb McKittrick Award as voted upon by his teammates.

Prior to joining the 49ers, Solari spent two seasons (2008–2009) as the offensive line coach for the Seattle Seahawks. Under his direction, tackle Walter Jones was selected to the Pro Bowl in 2008.

Following his initial stint with the 49ers, Solari spent nine seasons as the offensive line coach for Kansas City (1997–2005). With Solari directing the Kansas City offensive line, the team averaged 126.8 rushing yards per game, ranking fourth in the NFL during that time span.

Solari's line produced a trio of Pro Bowl offensive linemen in 2004 and 2005, in guards Will Shields and Brian Waters, as well as tackle Willie Roaf. Kansas City became the first club to accomplish that feat since Dallas from 1993 to 1996. As a result of his offensive line's dominance, the Chiefs offense led the league in total offense in 2004 (franchise record 418.4 ypg) and 2005 (387.0 ypg).

The Daly City, California, native was later promoted by the Chiefs to offensive coordinator in 2006. During his 11-year tenure in Kansas City, the team finished in the top 10 in rushing on seven occasions, in the top five four times, and ranked sixth in the NFL in total offense (359.2 yards per game) over that span. Solari was one of just six assistant coaches in team history to record more than a decade of service with the franchise.

While with the 49ers from 1992 to 1996, Solari was largely responsible for the development of tight end Brent Jones, who made four Pro Bowl appearances, and was instrumental in the team's successful Super Bowl XXIX season.

Solari began his NFL coaching career with the Dallas Cowboys in 1987, where he was the assistant offensive line/special teams coach for two seasons. He moved on to the Phoenix Cardinals to work with Gene Stallings for one season, before joining him at the University of Alabama (1990–1991).

In 1976, Solari's coaching career began at Mission Bay (CA) High School, followed by stints at Mira Costa Junior College (1978) and U.S. International (1979). The following year, he helped lead Boise State University to the NCAA Division I-AA championship. He spent additional time on the collegiate level at the University of Cincinnati (1981–1982) and the University of Kansas (1983–1985), and later served as the offensive coordinator at the University of Pittsburgh (1986).

A former offensive lineman at San Diego State University, Solari was a teammate of former Chiefs head coach and current ESPN analyst Herm Edwards, as well as Carolina Panthers head coach John Fox.

Solari and his wife, Patti, have three children, Tamara, Stephanie, and Michael.

Bob Wylie

THE FIRST MEETING WITH YOUR UNIT: LAYING THE GROUNDWORK FOR A SUCCESSFUL SEASON

Oakland Raiders

I am going to start out by showing you a four minute video. It is about the Oakland Raiders offensive line. We did not have an off-season program prior to the start of the season. They locked the players out of the NFL practice facilities.

We had four new coaches on the offensive staff. We had a new offensive coordinator. We did not run the offense that Hugh Jackson ran the previous year. We put in Al Saunders' offense, and we ran his offense. Al is a great offensive football coach. He has led the NFL in the number-one offense 12 different times. He has been coaching in the NFL 35 years. Al is a wonderful person to work with, and so is Hugh Jackson.

We did not have an off-season program, and we did not have a staff who had been together for several years, running the same offense. We had to start over again. We had to start from scratch. We did it the old-fashioned way. We did it the way Jim McNally did it when he started coaching in the NFL. Then, you saw the players at the mini-camp, and then you saw them again in July. We had to coach that way.

The film will show what we accomplished in a short period of time. After the film, I will tell you why we were able accomplish as much as we did in that short span of time. I will give you some statistics after we finish the film. (Film)

I showed you the film for a reason. As I said, we had no off-season program. Following are the things we accomplished with our offensive line last year.

We were 29th in sacks, and we finished in fourth place in the NFL. We were seventh in sacks per pass play. In the previous year, the average line rush was 3.1 yards on first down. This year, we rushed for 4.9 yards on first down. Our running back, Darren McFadden, led the league in rushing until he got hurt after seven games. We were second in runs of 20 yards and over. We tied for third on runs of 40 yards or more. We were tied for eight in runs of 50 yards or more. We reduced the number of hits on the quarterback from 121 to only 62 hits on the quarterback. We were 91 percent efficient on the goal line, and 86 percent efficient in short-yardage plays.

We were number-one in two-minute scoring. In all of the plays we ran in the two-minute offense, we only gave up two sacks. The offensive line only gave up 12 sacks and 25 as a total team. In week six, the offensive line received the Madden Protectors Award for their play against the Cleveland Browns. In that Cleveland Browns game, Stefen Wisniewski, a rookie, made the NFL Pro Football Weekly All-Rookie Team. Michael Bush ran for 977 yards and scored nine touchdowns, but only played in 10 games. He should have had at least 1,000 yards rushing. There were things we accomplished last season without an off-season program. People wanted to know how we accomplished this.

I am going to tell you how it all happened. I am going to start from the first time I meet the players. I am going to present the information to you, as I did to the players. You are here today, for our very first meeting as an offensive line. This is where we start.

There are things that happen in that first meeting that had to be a team concept. I met with the head coach and the offensive coordinator and discussed this as something we should teach our players. The staff bought into the ideas as it filtered into the offensive meeting rooms.

Following are some ideas I use with the offensive line:

The trouble with knowing everything is you can't learn anything new.

—Bill Muir's mother

Do the right things right.

—Dick Vermeil

Win: what is important now.

—Lou Holtz

Leave your ego at the door.

The first thing we tell everyone is: "Leave your ego at the door." Don't bring it to a game! We are all in this together. I am going to learn from the players, and the players are going to learn from me. Players have ideas, and I am willing to listen. There are certain things I want players to do that are the foundation of our concepts. We create the foundation for the program.

I give credit where credit is due. This next point comes from Bill Muir's mother: "The problem with knowing everything is you can't learn anything new." The point is this: The players do not know everything, and I do not know everything. If I do not have an answer to something, the players need to know that I will make sure we have that information by the time we get on the practice field. I will make sure that happens.

I want to add one additional part to this quote. "It is what you learn after you know everything that counts." When our daughter was growing up, I had a note on our refrigerator door that read like this: "Ask your teenagers now while they still know everything." This gets the point across to them.

This lets the players know that they do not know it all, and I do not know it all. But together, we are going to learn how to do things we need to know.

Dick Vermeil said, "Do right things right." It is a simple instruction. Do the right things right. Everyone here has their players stretch before practice. Watch your players stretch in practice. I will bet you any amount of money they are laying on the ground, talking to the players next to them, and they are trying to figure out what design the clouds are forming. They are stretching, but are they doing it the right way? Watch them as they stretch. Do right things right.

"Win! What is important now?" What is important right now at this moment? The toughest thing to teach players is to stay in the moment. I think this is true for any professional. It is difficult to teach players to stay in the moment. This is true in any sport.

What happens is this: We call a play. I have our offensive players organize their thoughts on the way to the line of scrimmage. The first question they must ask is this: "Who do I have to block?" Second: "What can the defense do to me from the configuration they line up in?" The third question is this: "How am I going to get the job done?" (i.e., What steps am I going to make? Am I going to step with the left or right foot first? Where am I going to put my helmet? Am I going to work with the center, or the tackle? What happens if we block down? How am I going to execute my assignment?)

On every play, they ask themselves those same three questions. They ask those questions on the way to the line of scrimmage, and not when they get down in their stance. If they wait until they get to the line of scrimmage, it is too late. On the way to the line of scrimmage, they must organize their thoughts.

The ball is snapped. "Win or lose the play! You make the block, or you do not make the block!" Now I am talking to you as an offensive line coach. You need to have a mindset where you get rid of the play. You learn from it.

When the whistle blows, it does not tell you to stop. It tells you to finish. You can be as upset with yourself as you want to be, but when you get back into the huddle and the quarterback calls, "I got it," you get rid of it. When the quarterback says, "I got it," you get rid of it. The quarterback is saying there is a starting and stopping point here. When he says, "I got it," you flush it. You get rid of it. You learn from it, and you get rid of it because it is lost in time forever. What is going to happen in the future, you have no idea. The only thing you can control is what is happening at this point right here and now. That is the only thing you have control of. One is lost forever, and the other you do not know about. The important thing is: "What is happening now?" Right now is what counts. You try to teach that to your players because the male ego takes over, and you win or lose the block.

When you lose, you worry about getting the defensive opponent the next play. We do not want players to worry about that situation. Instead, we want them to play the next play. "Play the next play!" This is the only thing that matters. You will hear me in practice yelling to the players, "Play the next play!" Forget the last play. There is nothing you can do about the last play. Play the next play. We will correct the mistakes on film in our meeting rooms. Play the next play. That is what is going to happen in a game.

COMMUNICATION

- Communication is the key to our success.
- I'm going to tell you what I expect from you. Learn how to turn it on and off.
- We will become excellent communicators.
- You will be tested on what you know at any time.
- I will coach what I know. I will not try to deceive you. If I don't know the answer, I will tell you. I will find the answer and give it to you before we go to practice.
- My job is to bring the Oakland Raiders offensive line together every single day and every single game.

WHAT AM I LOOKING FOR?

I have three questions I need to know about the players:

- Does the player know what to do?
- Is the player trying to do what the player is coached to do?
- Are they in shape? I am not playing! I have not played a snap in 40 years, and I do not intend to take a snap. The question is this: Are they in shape? Those are the things I am looking for in the players.

I go by what I see. You are what you see on tape. You can't hide anything. Coach Al Davis, God bless his soul, had cameras all over the place in training camp. He filmed the whole practice. You could not turn around in your drills without a camera filming the drill. He watched the entire practice.

If you do not know what to do, and if you are not doing what is coached, then we can't win with you. This is what I tell them in our very first meeting. We tell them we will find someone else we can win with. This is in our very first meeting with the players: *Football is a team sport and it is a game based entirely on situations. You must play at the highest level. Make a commitment! Team success is a perquisite to individual success.*

Football is based entirely on situations; red zone, short yardage, goal line, first down, second down, third down, third down and short, third down and long. The whole game is based on situations. What do I do in these situations? As coaches, we need to teach the players what to do in those situations.

THE FIRST FUNDAMENTAL OF FOOTBALL

There are no guarantees; you are playing in a high-performance game.

Last year, we lost the whole deal by one point! We lost the whole deal by a score of 29-28. Detroit went 98 yards on us and beat us 29-28. If we had kicked a field goal in the first quarter against the Lions, they would not have made the playoffs, right? The Bengals stay at home, right? Denver would not have won the AFC West because we would have won the AFC West.

That did not happen. For being at that height, I now have an unemployment card that the state of California gives you, so I can collect my $450 every week. So you can see the game is really tight. There are no guarantees in the game. However, you must play at a high-performance level.

COME TOGETHER THROUGH COMMUNICATION

Barriers of communication:
- Fear
- Habit
- Prejudice
- Language

These are barriers that players need to overcome. You get the players in a room, and they do not want to talk with each other. They are all afraid. There is prejudice against the rookies. Players do things by habit. You ask a player why he did something, and he will say it is the way he has always done it. It is a habit. Well, winning is a habit, and losing is a habit.

a habit. Well, winning is a habit, and losing is a habit. Also, players have different language skills.

The key to success is this:
- 80% Personal skill (communication, honesty, integrity)
- 20% Technical skill

We find that 80 percent of our life is based on communication. All of us in this room spend most of our time chasing techniques. "Which foot should I step with? Where do I put my hands? Where do my eyes go? Where should the center of gravity be on a block?" We are chasing things that happen only 15 to 20 percent of the time, instead of working on things that happen 80 percent of the time.

Players must communicate with each other. They must know the defense. The communication fact spreads from the line back to the quarterback. It spreads to the coaches on the sideline. It spreads up to the press box and back down to the coaches on the sideline. That is what you need to work on. Work on those things. Eighty percent of your life is based on this theory. We chase 20 percent of the things that we should not be chasing. Build in habits by always asking questions.

The 80 percent of success, the personal skills, should include:
- Communication
- Honesty
- Integrity

These are the three habits we are going to go with for the offensive linemen. We are going to communicate, we are going to be honest with one another, and we are going to have some integrity about it. When a player comes off to the sideline and I ask him if he blocked his man, I expect him to be honest about his answer. "I got him, Coach!" Then, when you watch the film on Monday morning, you see differently. I want to know exactly what is going on out on the field.

Build a filter system in your head to filter the four different kinds of communication:
- Phatic communication
  ✓ Small talk, a wave, casual meeting, introductions.
- Cathodic communication
  ✓ Negative, discontent, complaining.
- Persuasive communication
  ✓ Teaching, trying to move you in the right direction.
- Informative communication
  ✓ Information you can see. What I want you to do.

Be consistent as a player, and I will be consistent as a coach. There are four kinds of communication. In phatic communication, you may be walking down a hall and you see a player coming toward you. You greet the player with, "How are you doing?" His response is, "Great!" You keep on going down the hall. That is phatic communication.

Next is cathodic communication. It is kind of what your wife does when you get home late at night, right? "Why weren't you home at 5:00 p.m. for dinner?" It is not going to happen.

There is persuasive communication. It is trying to move the players in the right direction.

Then there is informative communication. It is communication you can see. It is what I want them to do. Those are the four types of communication.

Players must know when to turn it on, and when to turn it off. They have to know how to filter the good stuff and keep it, and when to filter the bad stuff and get rid of it. We talk about this in meetings. I tell them if they will be consistent as a player, I will be consistent as a coach.

Freedom to perform at the highest level of football is done through communication and preparation.

I expect you to have the highest standard of preparation! You will be tested.

I may walk into a locker room and ask them a question: "Center, how are we going to pick up that free safety blitz on 60 protection?" He better have an answer. It may be by a back adjusting his assignment, but he better have an answer.

LITTLE THINGS IN COMMUNICATION MAKE A DIFFERENCE

Example: "Wayne is down!" (Wrong.) We do not say that. Wayne is not down; that is negative. *He is not in the game.* We do not use the negative terms to describe players. We will build trust in one another. You will learn to think under pressure.

What do I mean when I say Wayne is down? We do not say Peyton Manning is down or our quarterback is down. We say, "Our quarterback is not in the game." There is a little different thought process that goes to the rest of the team. "Oh, crap! Peyton Manning is down. How in the hell are we going to win the game with him down?" That type of negative thought goes through the entire team. Peyton is down, but he may come back in the game. No! Peyton is not in the game is how we look at the situation. There is a different thought process here. How you communicate is important.

THE GAME IS SPONTANEOUS

Jazz sessions—This term comes from the North American Plains Indians. Following are examples of jazz sessions:
- Scoring a touchdown
- Kicking a field goal
- Interception for a touchdown
- Kickoff return for a touchdown
- Punt return for a touchdown

Go congratulate your buddy who scored. Celebrate with your teammates.

If you watched the Raiders last year, when we scored you could see the offensive linemen were the first players down to the end zone to congratulate the scorer. I kind of graded them on "Hollywood." When I stop a play at the end, I want them to be in that picture frame. "Are you in that picture when I stop the tape?" Get in Hollywood!

Celebrate with your buddies. I hate the guy who scores a touchdown and then points to himself and pounds on his chest as if he did everything to make the score possible. He does not recognize the fact that 10 other guys helped him get to the end zone for the score.

WORK TOGETHER

Gung Ho: To work in harmony together.

Shared Devotion to a Cause

What more shared devotion to a cause do we have as offensive line coaches than to get SOBs off of our quarterback? Why is this so important? In the NFL, when you start an offensive drive, you have 25 percent chance to score. That is it! It is a 25 percent chance to score either three points or six points. If you give up one sack, the chances go down to 4 percent. That is the difference when you give up a sack. That is why we work so hard to keep the quarterback from being sacked. We do not need the quarterback horizontal. We need for him to stay up.

Do some teams overcome that 4 percent? Yes! Some teams will drive the ball down the field after a sack, but the percentages are against you doing that.

Esprit De Corps: The common feeling that exists in members of a group and inspiring strong regard for the honor of that group.

The Dominant Feeling of the Battlefield Is That of Loneliness

The feeling you have for your teammates gets you through this feeling. In the Marines in combat, they do not care about the ground they are gaining, and they do not care if they are fighting for the USA against Iraq or whoever. Do you know what they care about the most? They care about the guy next to them? They care about getting that guy next to them out alive. How is that guy going to react? That is what they care about.

Your players need to think about the same thing. Think about the guy next to you. You need to know what he is going to do, before he does it. Sometimes, you cannot get the line call out, but you must know what the guy is going to do when the ball is snapped because the clock is running down. This is more important than which foot do I step with first on 16 Mike. *Esprit de corps gets you through it.*

Come Through for Your Teammates

Genghis Khan had an army of only 130,000 men, and they conquered over 5,500 miles in two and a half years. His horsemen could ride from 70 to 120 miles a day. They had tremendous endurance training. Every young man had to be an expert horseman and archer.

The Great Hunt was a drill that lasted three months. They drove the animals for 200 miles into a canyon. The archers went to kill the animals. They broke down into teams to see who was the best.

You talk about pressure, skills, and endurance; those guys could play. Those guys could hunt. That is what I want the offensive line to do.

GROUP CHEMISTRY

The group chemistry becomes the most important thing. It is more important than any blocking scheme.

What you create in your room with your players is more important than any X's and O's you can draw on the chalkboard. I am serious. This is not BS! The X's and O's are great, and we need them. We all know pro teams have playbooks that are six inches thick. The chemistry you create with your players in that meeting room is more important than those type things.

- I won't always have the answer.
- When something goes wrong, it is my fault. "You are my guys! I did not coach you well enough."
- I will refuse to let the offensive line be blamed without me being blamed.
- I will listen to your thoughts and ideas. I may not act on them, but I will listen to them. Players do come up with some good things.
- You need to be tough and tough-minded.

Everyone needs to improve their hands. All pro players play too high. I could look at the tapes of all of you here today and tell you what is wrong. All of the players need to improve their hands, and all of them play too high. There is not one coach in this room who escapes this problem.

We will, as an offensive line, do the following: We will be poised, physical, and finish everything we do!

I got that statement from Sam Wyche in the 1980s, when he coached the Bengals. We must be poised, as things are not going to go our way all of the time. We must teach the players to be poised. It is not always going to be perfect. They must learn to stay in the moment. They must be physical. We like physical players. Coach Paul Alexander likes physical players. We are not going to take one of those players who looks like a studio model jumping over the bags. You do not know if he can play or not.

- Treat people with courtesy on and off the field.
- There are no details too small.

If you want to get better, work a little harder.
—Jerry Rice

It is not rocket science, guys. If you want to be a better coach, work a little harder at it. If you want to be a better player, work a little harder.

BE KNOWN FOR SOMETHING

I like it when I hear our opponents say things about our line. "If you play against the Raiders, their offensive line does a super job of finishing their blocks." I like to hear that. Be known for something, okay? "Those guys can run block; those guys can pass block." It may just be being lined up straight across the line of scrimmage, or whatever it is, be known for something. "They look good getting off the bus." Be known for something.

The ability for you to play free and hard lies in the preparation that you put in.

MAKE A COMMITMENT TO FOUR THINGS

- Come off the ball. Your departure angle is critical.
- Step with the correct foot.
- Block the correct guy.
- Finish the block.

SIMPLE YET IMPORTANT INFORMATION

- We will learn to work in a demeanor.
- Wide base, knees bent in. Arch your back, feet on the ground turned out just a little on your instep. You want a base and an attitude.
- Learn to drive, lift, and push off with your instep, digging and pushing. You have anchor ability with your feet. Bend your knees, and sink your hips.
- When you are blocking the linebacker, bend your knees and get a base on contact. When you bend your knees and bring them together, your butt sinks. You can't do enough with your feet spread. You have to gather yourself before you strike.
- Be under control. Have an attitude. Train yourself to have body control.

- The toughest game we play is against our own guys. Get the best picture on the practice field.

You should get with the person who is drawing up the play cards for the scout team to see what they are facing when they go against the first team. You want to get the best practice picture you can get from those cards. You want a good look at what you are going to see on Sunday.

POWER OF THE OBJECTIVE: ACHIEVE COMPETITIVE GREATNESS

- Great is a sense of destiny.
- No matter who you are, no matter what you do, leave your mark.
- You must have a clean-cut objective. Then, you must have a step-by-step progression on how you are going to achieve that objective.

That may be just coming to practice every day. What are you going to give them as an objective for that day? It may be to improve the inside hand on one play. It may be to step with the correct foot on a pass play. Give them something that day that they do not do well, so at the end of the day when you look at the tape, they have gotten better. It does not have to be a lot. It can be a small thing for that day, which may be good enough.

I have really bought into this next concept.

UNCONSCIOUS COMPETENCE

- John F. Kennedy said, "We choose to go to the moon. We choose to go to the moon not because it is easy, but because it is hard."
- Socrates an ancient Greek believed in unconscious competence.

Four Stages of Learning a New Skill

Everyone in this room learns this way. I started looking at this idea about six to eight years ago. I wish I had known these things earlier in my career. No one gets behind the way you learn here. You want to get to unconscious competence, but you have to go through these steps:

1. Unconscious incompetence: The player has no idea of the skill.
2. Conscious incompetence: The player becomes aware of the skill.
3. Conscious competence: The player can perform the skill reliable at will.
4. Unconscious competence: Skill so practiced that it enters the unconscious part of the brain. It becomes second nature.

I tell the players I am going to teach them things they have never learned before. We teach them the new techniques and skills. In order to make the players better, you must be able to show them where they are deficient. When you show them the new skills, you show them how that skill is going to make them better.

The point comes to where the skills exist in the players. The player is incompetent because he does not know how to do the skill. That is the second stage.

In the third stage, the player can perform the skills, but he still has to think about it. If he has to think about his first step (hit and lift), then he has not accomplished our goal. We must get him to stage four of unconscious competence, where the skills become second nature.

How many of you drove here today? Raise your hand. Did you think about it? No. You got in your car, put your seatbelt on, and you drove here. You did not have to think about it. How many of you here went to the bathroom this morning and turned on the light on? Did you think about it? No. It is your subconscious. You just did it.

You need to get your players to play like that. It cannot be from stage 2 to stage 4 or from stage 1 to stage three 3. It must be from stages 1, 2, 3, and 4.

Coaches commonly assume the player is a stage 2 and focus efforts toward achieving stage 3, when often the players are still at stage 1.

The coach assumes the player is aware of the skill of existence, nature, relevance, deficiency, and benefit offered from the acquisition of the new skill, whereas players at stage 1 (unconscious incompetence) have none of these things in place and will not be able to address achieving conscious competence until they become conscious and fully aware of their own incompetence. This is a fundamental reason for the failure of a lot of coaching and teaching.

If the awareness of a skill and deficiency is low or non-existent (i.e., the players are not at the unconscious incompetence stage), then the players will simply not see the need for learning. It is essential to establish awareness of a weakness or need (conscious incompetence) prior to attempting to impart or arrange the skills necessary to move the players from stage 2 to stage 3.

MANAGE YOUR BEHAVIOR TO MEET THE CHALLENGE AT HAND

- Great teams are:
  ✓ Aggressive
  ✓ Competent
  ✓ Discipline
- Inspiration comes from everybody
- People who produce great results feel good about themselves.
- *Power of endurance:* Inside all of us is an extraordinary person waiting to be released. Unless you go past your personal best, you will never unleash that person.
- *Delta Force:* Makes you go through the process called selection, and you live in the world of suck.
- *Football is a high performance business:*
  ✓ Men who have talent who don't use it fail.
  ✓ Men who have talent and use it half fail.
  ✓ Men who have talent and use it to its fullest extent will experience satisfaction beyond no other that few men will ever know.
- Get players to go past their personal best. That is what coaches must strive for working with players.

PAIN—TWO KINDS

- *Discipline:* The pain of discipline is temporary.
- *Regret:* The pain of regret lasts a lifetime.

I run our guys on gassers after practice. They start at the 15-yard line, and they run gassers back and forth across the field. Do they run the gassers to get into shape? No! That has nothing to do with it. I have them run because I want to see how mentally tough they are. I want them to line up and to be disciplined. I want their foot on the line, run across the field and touch the line, and come back to the starting point. I do not want them to finish early. I want them to finish on the line. I want to see how mentally tough they can become. That is pain of discipline. That pain is going to go away. They can go in and get in a hot tub, or a cold tub, and then take a shower. That pain is going to subside, and it is going to go away.

The pain of regret lasts a lifetime. Say you are playing in the Super Bowl, and you are supposed to block the noseguard, but you turn outside and block the defensive end, and the noseguard makes the tackle and your team loses the Super Bowl. The pain for that mistake will last a lifetime.

If you are a running back and you fumble the football, and a defender picks up the football and runs it back for a touchdown, and you lose the game. That pain last a lifetime.

LEARN TO WORK AT A HIGH LEVEL THROUGH HABIT

Develop your technique so it is faster than the other guy, have better leverage, finish longer, play harder, and be poised. When your life is on the line you have to have courage. Without fear there can be no courage. You must have discipline and trust in your body. You have to make it happen.

HEADMAN MOLEFHE MANGADI: "ALWAYS GET THE FIGHT STARTED IN SMALL GROUPS."

Get the fight started in your room. I watch my players. You say don't fight on a football field. In training camp, if we do not get into a fight with the defensive linemen, there is a problem. If I see my guys fighting, I keep an eye on them. If my guys are on top, I do not break it up. Really, I am not going to break it up, anyway.

POINTS OF LEADERSHIP

- Communication
- Self-control
- High standards
- Tolerance and patience
- Decisiveness
- Social poise

- Trust
- Ability to organize time and priorities
- Intense desire to compete
- Consideration of others
- Enthusiasm
- Timeliness

If you have a problem, you will attack the problem and keep the person out of it.

Know the players. Somebody in his life is more powerful than you. Know your players, and find out who that person is. If you have a problem, you may have to call his Pop Warner football coach because that player has more control over the players than you do. Find out who that guy is.

MY THOUGHTS ON LEADERSHIP

I am not going over these points. This is 66 thoughts on leadership. I am not going over them. If anyone wants this material, just give me your email address, and I will email you the entire list.

This is what I do in our first meeting with the players. It is what I go through with the players. I do not talk about the techniques. I talk about this stuff in our very first meeting. To me, this is more important than the techniques. It took me a long time to learn this. This showed up when I coached up in Canada. I covered the same material. Some of the players did not speak fluent English, but they got what I was trying to get across to them.

Last year was a great example of the whole ball of wax. We had a new offense. We had new coaches on offense. We finished ninth in offense in the NFL. They bought into the system. The communication was fantastic.

My time is up, and I am going to turn the program over to Paul Alexander. Thank you for your attention.

ABOUT THE AUTHOR

Bob Wylie, who has more than 30 years of coaching experience, was named the Oakland Raiders offensive line coach on February 1, 2011. During his first year with the Raiders, the offensive line improved from 29th in the NFL in 2010 to fourth in 2011 in total sacks allowed and seventh in sacks per pass play. The line also improved in rushing yards from 3.1 yards on first down to 4.9 yards and had the leading rusher after the first six games in running back Darren McFadden. The Raiders finished the season ranked seventh in total rushing yards, second in number of 20+ yard rushing plays, and tied for third in rushing plays of over 40 yards.

The offensive line received the Madden Protectors Award in week 6 for their performance against the Cleveland Browns, and rookie guard Stefen Wisniewski was named to the PFW All-Rookie Team. They also paved the way for running back Michael Bush to rush for 977 yards and seven touchdowns.

Prior to his position with the Raiders, Wylie was the offensive line coach for the Denver Broncos (2010). With the Broncos, the offensive line ranked sixth in the NFL, averaging 4.7 yards per carry, during the second half of the season. The club's second-half rushing yards per game improvement of 58.6 yards per game ranked second in the league.

Wylie joined the Broncos after working as an offensive line coach in the Canadian Football League with Saskatchewan (2009) and Winnipeg (2007–2008). Wylie owns the unique distinction of instructing at five different levels of football. He has coached at the Pop Warner, junior high school, high school, college, and professional levels.

During his three years as an offensive line coach in the Canadian Football League, Wylie was part of two teams that played in the Grey Cup: Saskatchewan (2009) and Winnipeg (2007). Believed to be the only assistant coach in CFL history to appear on two Grey Cup teams within his first three years in the league, Wylie coached players to All-Star appearances at every offensive line position (tackle, guard, and center) in the CFL.

Despite four starters missing significant portions of time, Wylie's offensive line with Saskatchewan in 2009 helped the club rank near the top of several offensive statistical categories en route to winning its first division title in 33 years. His effort with the Roughriders followed two years coaching a Winnipeg offensive line that allowed the fewest sacks in the CFL from 2007 to 2008, leading the league in 2007 and ranking second in 2008 while using 14 different starters over the stretch.

Before coaching the offensive line at Syracuse University from 2005 to 2006, Wylie spent eight consecutive years coaching in the NFL. He instructed the Cardinals' offensive line in 2004 with his unit blocking for the NFL's all-time leading rusher, Emmitt Smith, during his final pro season. From 1999 to 2003, Wylie coached the Bears offensive line and helped the club allow an NFL-low 17 sacks in 2001 that propelled the team to an NFC Central title. Bears center Olin Kreutz earned three consecutive Pro Bowl selections (2001–2003) under Wylie while tackle James Williams was named to his first Pro Bowl of his career in 2001.

Wylie's offensive line also helped Chicago running back Anthony Thomas to earn Associated Press NFL Offensive Rookie of the Year honors after he rushed for 1,183 yards in 2001. Thomas's effort marked the seventh time a player totaled at least 1,000 rushing yards in a season with Wylie on staff.

From 1997 to 1998, Wylie was the Bengals tight ends coach and oversaw a group that blocked for running back Corey Dillon, who broke the NFL single-game rushing record, during his consecutive 1,000-yard rushing seasons. He had a one-year stint as the University of Cincinnati's offensive line coach in 1996, a year in which the Bearcats led the Conference USA in rushing and featured four linemen who earned postseason honors, including tackle Jason Fabini. Fabini was one of five players coached by Wylie selected in the NFL Draft.

During four seasons as Tampa Bay's offensive line coach from 1992 to 1995, Wylie's group helped running back Errict Rhett become only the fifth player in NFL history to post consecutive 1,000-yard rushing seasons in his first years in the league (1994–1995). He also coached Pro Football Hall of Fame tackle Anthony Muñoz in training camp in 1993, his final pro season.

Wylie's NFL coaching career began with a two-year stint as the Jets tight ends coach from 1990 to 1991. Before entering the NFL coaching ranks, Wylie coached for 10 seasons at the collegiate level, handling offensive line duties at Brown University (1980–1982), College of the Holy Cross (1983–1984), and Colorado State University (1988–1989) in addition to working as offensive coordinator at Ohio University (1985–1987). At CSU, he worked under NCAA Hall of Fame Coach Earle Bruce.

A native of West Warwick, Rhode Island, Wylie was a teacher and administrator in his hometown from 1973 to 1980. Wylie played linebacker at the college level in Colorado for three years before transferring to Roger Williams College, where he received a bachelor's degree in American studies. He also earned a master's degree in economics from the University of Rhode Island in 1975.

Inducted into the West Warwick High School Hall of Fame in 1999, Wylie received the NFL's Extra Effort Award in 2001 for his work with Chicago-area youth. He is also one of the organizers of the annual Offensive Line Clinic that takes place in Cincinnati and features some of the nation's top coaches.

A licensed pilot and amateur magician, Wylie was born on February 16, 1951, and he has one daughter (Jennifer) and one grandson (Wylie).

WYLIE AT A GLANCE

- 2011-present: Oakland Raiders, Offensive Line
- 2010: Denver Broncos, Assistant Offensive Line
- 2009: Saskatchewan Roughriders (CFL), Offensive Line
- 2007-2008: Winnipeg Blue Bombers (CFL), Offensive Line
- 2005-2006: Syracuse University, Offensive Line
- 2004: Arizona Cardinals, Offensive Line
- 1999-2003: Chicago Bears, Offensive Line
- 1997-1998: Cincinnati Bengals, Tight Ends
- 1996: University of Cincinnati, Offensive Line
- 1992-1995: Tampa Bay Buccaneers, Offensive Line
- 1990-1991: New York Jets, Tight Ends
- 1988-1989: Colorado State University, Offensive Line
- 1985-1987: Ohio University, Offensive Coordinator
- 1983-1984: College of the Holy Cross, Offensive Line
- 1980-1982: Brown University, Offensive Line

George Yarno

FIVE- AND SIX-MAN PROTECTION TECHNIQUES AND DRILLS

Detroit Lions

That 90-yard drive Bob Wylie was talking about in the Detroit/Oakland game was the result of many good athletes. We had Calvin Johnson and Matthew Stafford. All the offensive line had to do was get in the way of the rush long enough.

It is nice to be here, and I appreciate you coaches taking time out of your schedule to make yourselves better. I listened to all the coaches who talked last night and today. I got something from everyone of them. If I can give you one or two things that help you, it will be awesome.

Football is a very intense, emotional, and draining game. When players come into our meeting room, I want them to learn. I want them to be comfortable, and I do not want them to think I am going to put them up on display. I am going to take care of them because I want them to learn. The only way to learn is to communicate.

I want to tell you a little about my history. I was fortunate enough to play 13 years of professional football. I was a defensive lineman in college. They converted me to offense when I went to the NFL with Tampa Bay back in the early 1970s. My first offensive line coach was a coach named Bill "Tiger" Johnson.

Two years ago, Howard Mudd was here at this clinic speaking. He went over the 26 points of what every offensive line coach should know. I wrote those down and put them in my notebook. I thought it was great because he did not use any high technology in his presentation. He just talked.

I learned from a coach who sort of revolutionized football. Back when Tiger played, you could not extend your arms. You could bring your thumbs up to your chest and have the forearms in front of you. That was the blocking posture in that day. When he taught pass blocking, he taught players to bring their forearms up in a boxer's posture with the forearms framing the face and the fists up in the air. He did that because the head slap was a legal move. The defensive lineman came off the line of scrimmage and tried to put his fist through the offensive blocker's earhole on the helmet.

My rookie season, we played the Washington Redskins in an exhibition game. Washington had a great defensive lineman by the name of Diron Talbert. The game was in the third quarter, and he was mad because he was still on the field in an exhibition game. He was a veteran lineman and felt he should not be on the field in the third quarter of an exhibition game. He was mad, so he took his anger out on me.

This was the first year they outlawed the head slap. We called a pass, and I sat up to pass block with my hands down. He came across the line of scrimmage and met me with a three-punch combination to the helmet. I went to my knees. He stood over me and said, "Welcome to the NFL." He did not even rush the quarterback. I staggered back to the huddle, thinking I could maybe get a job at Wal-Mart.

In my 13-year career, I was with a number of teams and had several good line coaches. Tiger Johnson taught me to see the game from the big picture. He taught me to see all the pieces and how they fit together. My next offensive line coach was a coach name Kim Helton. He was an emotional, tempo-oriented, tough guy. I got some of my coaching values from him. The next coach was Larry Beightol, and he was a technician and still is. He taught you the balance of the game. He taught how to coil your joints to strike a player.

The next offensive line coach I had was Jim Hanifan. He had some unbelievable drills and had a good outlook at the game. We did the sandbag drills. It was not like the sandbags they have in the game today. He had a burlap sack, went to the hardware store, filled it up with sand, and had someone sew it up. That was in Atlanta. He did the sandbag drill, and the sand ended up in your face and throat. However, he helped to develop offensive linemen mentally and physically.

The last coach I played for was Charlie Johnson. I was with him at Green Bay. He installed the terms and assignment rules that made perfect sense to me. I still use them to this day, and I will show them to you in a few minutes. He believed you learned football. You did not memorize it. That is true. You cannot be good at something if you memorize it. It is only good for the limited area that you have that information. If you learn something, the defense cannot keep you from getting a hat on a hat.

If you learn it, you can get back to the line of scrimmage. Second-and-10 does not kill you. Zero yardage plays do not beat you. What beats you is linemen blowing assignments and turning defenders loose. That is when you lose the quarterback for the season or turn the ball over.

I was fortunate enough to have a bunch of outstanding offensive line coaches to mentor me. I was a clean slate because I was a defensive player my entire college career. I learned the offensive side of the ball through those coaches. My assistant line coach is Jeremiah Washburn. He is sitting back there and needs all your sympathy. Kyle Valero, our offensive assistant, is sitting up here. They did a great job of helping me and putting all the video together. I am an old school coach, and all the technology is new to me.

I sat through all the meetings we have had at this clinic and heard the same thing from each coach. They all say there is no one way to do things. There are different ways to teach the same thing. There is no one right way to block a defender. There are many good ways, but the right way is what you believe in and what works for you.

You can take the information we share with you, tweak it, and use what works for you. If you get something of interest out of this conversation, that is great. That is why I am here. I am here to help you pick up one or two little things that will make you a better coach.

Everything I know, I learned from someone else. I did not invent this stuff. I have never invented anything. I am a copycat. However, I took the things that I believed in, put it together, and made it my system.

I adhere to the KISS theory. Football is a simple game made difficult by egos. Everybody thinks he is smarter than anyone else. Coaches cannot let their egos get in the way of their coaching. It does not matter what the coach knows. It does not matter what your player knows. It is what your player can execute that is important. We keep the techniques very simple. I coached college football for 17 years before I got in to the NFL. I have always tried to keep the techniques as simple as possible.

I am a "why" coach. I want the players to know why we are doing the things we do. The reason we want to keep it simple is that the balance a lineman has is totally learned. It is not natural athletic balance. The natural athletic balance for an athlete is shoulders over the toes with the knees bent. It does not matter if you swing a golf club, baseball bat, or a croquet mallet. The balance for the offensive line in the run game is shoulders over knees, chest on the thighs, and knees over the toes.

Pass protection balance is worse. The shoulders are over the mid-thigh with the knee over the ball of the foot. You cannot stay in that position for any length of time. It is unnatural. We learn balance as offensive linemen because he is the only athlete who plays a game with a ball or object where he plays with his back to the ball. That makes the offensive lineman the most unique and special athlete on the face of the earth.

I want my players to believe that. Being an offensive lineman is an unnatural position. You have to do things to make an unnatural process feel as natural as you can. That is why I am constantly looking for drills. The drills you use make an unnatural practice natural. I will show you some of the drills we use with the rookie as we travel along on our journey today.

You want your players to take pride in what they do. We do many youth league camps with small kids. In those camps, you have 200 players. We have 12 offensive linemen and 150 quarterbacks. I get to coach the fat, dumpy kids who cannot do anything else. The reason for that is no one wants to be an offensive lineman. You have to instill a sense of pride in your group.

I know there is about half and half college to high school coaches represented here today. I know you guys are under time constrains. Every level you get to, the more time you get with the players. During the season, I get my players for four hours of meetings a day. We have time to coach all the small personal details of each player. We can work on the unique habits of a defender. In high school, you may get two hours a week with your players if you are lucky. In college, you get about 45 minutes a day.

That means you have to teach an unnatural position in a limited amount of time. The offensive line has to work as a single unit. As one lineman goes, they all go. You have to tie that together in 45 minutes a day or two hours a week. To do that, you must keep it simple. You cannot ask too much from your players. It is what they can execute, not what they know. Sometimes, the ego gets in the way, and you try to do too much. If you give the players too much, you overload them. At the same time, while you are teaching, you want your players to grow in their skills and ability.

Most of the high school coaches are probably teachers, too. You know that everyone learns differently. We have a player who has ADD on one side and a player who went to Stanford on the other side. You have a player who went to a trade school and mastered in basket weaving. However, it does not matter because you have to teach everyone. I have 12-year veterans sitting in the back of the room, waiting for me to give them something. You have to get everyone to grow.

You have to find a way so that everyone can grow. That is why I believe in my rules. There are four basic rules in blocking. I can block any play in the world with a combination of these rules. The first rule is man blocking.

MAN BLOCK

This is a simple counting rule (Diagram #1). The center has the 0 defender. The guard has the #1 defender. The tackle has the #2 defender. The tight end has the #3 defender. The backside guard has #1, and the backside tackle has the #2 defender. The center must declare the 0 defender so the counting process can start. The initial MDM stands for "most dangerous man" on your side.

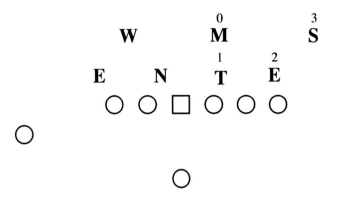

Diagram #1. Counting 4-3 Stack

This is a simple counting procedure (Diagram #2). We use it because the defenders are all over the place in their defensive alignments. It does not matter their position or the number they wear; we will declare who they are in relationship to our blocking scheme. The 0 declaration by the center is a count from the outside going to the inside of the alignment. The count depends on how many blockers you have to a particular side. If we have a guard, tackle, and tight end to one side, we have three blockers to that side, and the center is the fourth blocker. Counting from the outside, the center is responsible for the fourth defender or the apex of the defense to that side. That defender is the 0 defender.

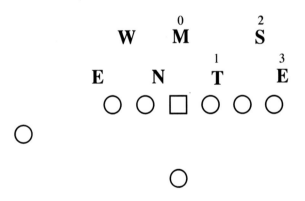

Diagram #2. Counting 4-3

When the center declares the 0 defender, he calls out his number and points at him. He points at someone every play. That way, it does not tell the defense anything we are doing. If we run the inside zone play, the center comes to the line of scrimmage and declares, "Mike 52." The next play is a dropback pass. The center comes to the line and declares, "Mike 52." It is the same declaration, but it is a different play. The defense cannot read what you do from the declaration.

The offense does not want to tip what they are doing particularly with a stance tip. It makes no difference whether the offensive lineman is in a two- or three-point stance. I do not care as long as they can function. You cannot let the defender know what you are doing before you snap the ball. The offensive players have two advantages. They know the snap count, and they know where the ball is going.

We added the MDM two years ago (Diagram #3). This is a designation when the fourth blocker comes from the backfield. We have five defenders, which mean we have a fourth blocker in the backfield who will block one of those defenders. In the NFL, we do not block anyone coming out of the backfield who aligns on the line of scrimmage. The reason we do not do that is because that player is going to get the crap knocked out of him, and the play will be unsuccessful. In Diagram #3, the 0, #1, #2, and #3 are on the line of scrimmage. The #4 defender is the linebacker off the line of scrimmage, and he is the defender assigned to the back coming out of the backfield.

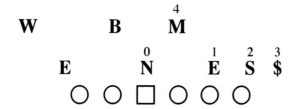

Diagram #3. Counting 3-4 MDM

BIG BLOCK

This is big-on-big blocking. The guard and tackle block the two level one defenders to their side on the line of scrimmage. If there is only one defensive lineman on your side, go back to the man rule. Level one is the defensive linemen, and level two is the linebacker level.

The first diagram is a 4-3 under defense (Diagram #4). With the big rules, the 3 technique defender is the #1 first-level defender and belongs to the guard. The 5 technique is the #2 first-level defender and belongs to the tackle. The Will linebacker is the

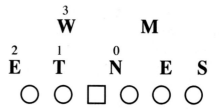

Diagram #4. Big 4-3 Under

#3 defender and blocked by the back coming out of the backfield. When we block a big play, the third blocker comes out of the backfield.

The second situation is a 3-4 alignment to the big side (Diagram #5). In the NFL, the Will linebacker in the diagram is a pass rusher. We do not want the back to block a glorified defensive lineman. It is a mismatch. The guard and tackle block the 5 technique and the Will linebacker. The back takes the soft rusher or MDM. In this example, the MDM is the Mike linebacker.

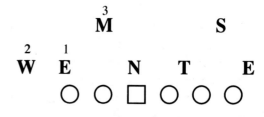

Diagram #5. Big 3-4

If we get an overload to the weakside, it is a bad situation (Diagram #6). The #1, #2, and #3 defenders are all on the line of scrimmage. The Mike linebacker becomes the 0 defender, and the center has to block him. We never put the center on the MDM. If we tried to reach the center to the nose, the guard to the defensive end, and the tackle to the Will linebacker, the defense has the advantage. The defense crushes anything run to this side and pushes it back into the backfield. We block the nose

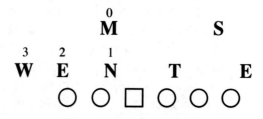

Diagram #6. Big Overload

with the guard, the end with the tackle, and the back takes the Will linebacker. The center takes the Mike linebacker, and we get a hat on a hat.

In Diagram #4, if the Will linebacker walked up into the A gap, he becomes a level one player, and we count him as #1 on the line. The guard blocks the linebacker, the tackle blocks the 3 technique defender, and the running back takes on the defensive end. I hope that the quarterback takes us out of the play. If he does not, we get a hat on a hat. That is better than letting the linebacker run free through the A gap and cause a turnover. Second-and-10 for the first down does not kill you. The turnover is what can be a drive-killer or game-turner.

I am never going to let a linebacker run through the A or B gap unblocked. It is not going to happen. We will scheme and never let that happen.

GAP BLOCK

You are responsible for a gap or an area, *not* a defender. If your gap is not threatened, you block man on, which will create a double-team. You want the double-team to be as close to the hole as you can. In the running game, you are responsible for an area to a man (Diagram #7). The blockers can go down field so they double-team to a linebacker. On a power play, you have five blockers to the playside of the play. That means the center works to the backside of the play. The center determines his 0 declare by the number of blockers there are to the playside.

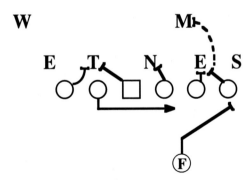

Diagram #7. Gap Power Play

The center still makes a 0 designation, although it does not mean anything. He knows he goes to the backside on the power. On an occasion, the 0 declaration on a power play could mean something.

DUAL RULE

The two blockers on a side are responsible for the three potential rushers (3-on-2). You block two most dangerous rushers and double bump for the third. The guard has A gap bump, and the tackle has B gap bump.

In this situation, two linemen have an extra rusher for which they are responsible. Someone has a dual responsibility on most pass protections. It may not be the offensive line, but someone in the protection scheme has a dual responsibility. It could be the quarterback reading two defenders and throwing hot.

With three potential rushers and two blockers, the blockers always block the most dangerous men (Diagram #8). The linemen block the two most dangerous rushers, and if they all come, the quarterback is responsible for the third rusher.

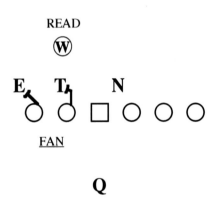

Diagram #8. Dual Rule Fan

In the rules, I have A gap bump and B gap bump. I dropped that. In the NFL, if you try to block two defenders, you end up blocking 0 defenders. We block one, and he is the most dangerous one. If the guard blocks on the most dangerous and a linebacker runs through the B gap, he might be able to get a hand on him, but he does not bump over and try to block him. He does not release the defender he is blocking to block a blitzing linebacker. The quarterback reads him and throws hot.

If the Will linebacker shows up in the A gap in his alignment, he is the most dangerous man to the guard (Diagram #9). The tackle squeezes down on the 3 technique tackle, and the guard takes the Will linebacker. The quarterback reads the defensive

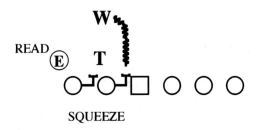

Diagram #9. Dual Rule Squeeze

end for his hot throw. If they run a zone blitz and the tackle drops out of the line of scrimmage in a pass drop, the tackle bails out and blocks on the defensive end. If the Will linebacker drops off the line of scrimmage, the guard bails out and blocks the defensive end.

You can draw up any defense you want, and I can block you assignment-wise with one of the four rules or a combination of them. If we can master those four things, we can get a hat on a hat in any defense.

The information about a play is what I call "parts to the puzzle." The terminology you use in the huddle and at the line of scrimmage is information that each position takes in and decides what to do with it. We take the pieces of the puzzle, put them together, and form the big picture. That is why you give them information in the huddle so they can understand what to do on the play. The words and numbers should trigger pictures in the minds of the offensive linemen.

The next thing I want to cover is a pass pro concept. The first thing is six-man protection. Before I get to that, I want to cover one more thing. You need to be consistent with what you put into your playbook. If you use word terms to mean runs, the number terms should be passes. It does not matter which way you do it.

If the receiver coach uses numbers to define his patterns, you should use words to call the protection. An example would be jet right 686. If the receiver coach or quarterback coach likes words for pass combinations, the protection scheme should be numbers. A California pattern is a curl/flat combination. Your play call is California 62. What you do not want to do is have number for both the protection scheme and the patterns. You do not want to call "62-695." The linemen will think they are getting the combination to their locker.

The playbook has to develop a system. If you use the term jet, it means the same thing throughout the entire playbook. It is important to set up the system so it is learner-friendly. We do not want to memorize the playbook; we want to learn what is in it. If you memorize, the player are playing with blinders on their eyes. They have to understand and see the big picture, not just the limited vision. The pieces must fit together consistently.

I do not want my coaches to be in a position to have to say, "Because I said so." When a player asks "Why," I want to tell him why.

In pass protection, when you develop your system, the numbers and word terms should answer three questions:

- How many blockers do you have? What are their assignments?
- Where is the quarterback setting up? Where is his launch point?
- Who do we have? What are the assignments for offensive line?

You have to know how many blockers are involved in the protection. Is it a five-, six-, seven-, or eight-man protection? After we know the number of blockers, we must know what they are doing. We have to define the assignments of extra blockers in the overall protection scheme. If there is a back or tight end involved in the scheme, whom are they blocking? It is not good enough to know what you are doing. You must know what the other people are doing as well if you are going to learn the game of football for an offensive lineman.

If the offensive lineman does not know the running back is blocking to the weakside on six-man protection, he will get someone hurt. I cannot put that player on the field. When we make mistakes, people get hurt, games are lost, the season gets lost, and we end up going to the U-Haul® place again. The offensive line cannot get beat mentally.

We must know the point at which the quarterback throws the ball. We also need to know how the quarterback is getting to that point. We must know if it is play-action, in the gun, under center, dropback, or some other method of dropping. In our protection scheme, we have a quick, pocket, and drop protections. The quick protection is the three-step drop. The pocket protection is the five-step drop (seven yards). The drop protection is nine yards deep.

The linemen must know the launch point of the quarterback because it affects the way the offensive lineman sets. The shortest distance between two points is a straight line. That is one other reason I like the game of football. It is logical and mathematical. The game is leverage, angles, and trajectory. Some people think the English language is a second language for me. However, I understand it well.

The direct line between the quarterback's launch point and the defender is important. The defender, blocker, and quarterback are in a straight line. The offensive tackle wants to set to the direct line between the defender and the quarterback. That is a simple goal, but he has to do it with balance. He has to have an inside-out position. In his set, he wants his weight over the middle of his inside groin muscle. The shoulder is over the mid-thigh with the knee over the ball of the foot.

The next-quickest way to the quarterback for the defender is to the inside. That is why we take that path away from him. The blocker wants the defender to go outside so he can flatten him when he does. It is hard to get into that position and be in balance. That position is an unnatural balance. It is hard for an offensive lineman to sit in an unnatural position, punch the rusher, and stop his momentum. That is why they pay offensive linemen so well in the NFL. It is hard to find a good one.

That leads me to the next point. I used to say, "Punch" all the time. I use the term "stab" now. The new term is "stab and grab." The offensive lineman stabs the defender and grabs him. Howard Mudd coached my brother in the NFL, and I have known him for 30-plus years. He asked his players all the time why God gave people thumbs. He gave you thumbs so you can grab things. We want to get a hold of the rusher and make him drag our dead carcass back to the quarterback. Since the offensive linemen are just a bunch of huge guys, it will take him a while to do it.

When you teach the stab from the set, you teach eyes up, thumbs up, and palms up. I tell them eyes up, thumbs up, palms up, and strike up. I try to use sayings that create pictures in their minds.

If the eyes go down, the head goes down, and the lineman loses his balance. To regain his balance, he must step back, which opens his hips to the outside.

The offensive lineman uses the stab to stop the momentum of the rusher and maintain his balance. He does not have to stop the momentum; he can redirect the rusher momentum toward the quarterback. You know you have accomplished that goal when the defender's feet stop going to the quarterback and he takes another path. If his feet continue to go toward the quarterback, the blocker has not stopped the momentum of the rusher. He has accepted the momentum of the rusher, and the rusher controls the blocker's balance. We work those fundamentals every day.

I played with a player by the name of Bruce Matthews. He played 19 years in the NFL and is a Hall of Fame lineman. I was fortunate enough to play between Bruce Matthews and Mike Munchak. Bruce had unbelievable balance. He was heavy handed and strong. However, his feet were all over the place. He was a great player, but he was not perfect in his technique. No one ever gets it done perfectly. The only thing you can do is work toward that type of perfection. You are trying to teach them how to strike, when to strike, and how to maintain the balance.

The most natural thing to do when you try to stab someone is to lead with the head and shoulders. It is hard to keep your head up, eyes up, and get your hands up.

Hand placement is an important part of the technique. I want the hands carried above the belt line. I want them into the body and not out in front. I want the thumbs up and the hands in a relaxed position. The worst thing you can do is tense up before you strike a defender. If you do, you lose all your power.

We want the thumbs up because it brings the elbows tight to the rib cage. The power in your body comes from the joints. In the old hand winches, there were combinations of wheels and pulleys that the cables ran through that lifted the heavy weights with no difficulty. The joints of the body are like that winch system. The wrist, elbow, and shoulder are all pulleys in the body. You must get them in a straight line. The angle, knees, and hips are the same process in the lower part of the body. The more you can align those joints, the more power you have.

The important point about flexibility is in ankle flexion. The lineman has to be able to get his knee over the ball of his foot with his foot flat on the ground. If the lineman does not have a flexible ankle, the knee goes over the heel. When that happens, the body goes up, and we start to lose the leverage battle.

I want to get into six-man protection. We call that protection "jet right/left or 62/63." The first question we ask is: How many blockers? We have six pass blockers in six-man protection. The five offensive linemen and the running back are the players involved in the scheme. In jet right protection, the running back goes to the right side of the formation and blocks the Mike or Sam linebacker. The tight end releases on this protection scheme.

In the jet scheme, the quarterback has pocket protection. That means he is seven yards deep in his drop. The five offensive linemen in jet protection block the four down defender and the Will linebacker. The offensive line must use their rules to carry out their assignment.

If the formation has the tight end on the right side and the running back blocking to that side, the right tackle and guard's rule is big (Diagram #10). The center and left guard and tackle block gap rule. The center's rule would be the Will linebacker. Since he is removed from the immediate area of the center's alignment, the center blocks the A gap. The guard and tackle to the left side block the B and C gaps to that side.

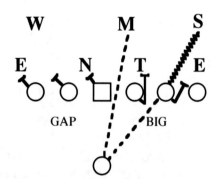

Diagram #10. Jet Right Big Gap

The center points out the Mike linebacker, which means nothing in the protection scheme.

After he does that, he gives a slide call. In this case, the call is "Lou." The center makes the call; however, the left guard and tackle should echo the call. If someone makes a mistake, we all make a mistake. The worst thing the lineman can say when we get to the sideline after a negative play is, "He did not make the call."

The offensive linemen have a nomenclature they use at the line and in the huddle. Nomenclature is a working vocabulary for the linemen. The words the linemen use during the heat of the battle are their nomenclature.

An adjustment we might use is if the Sam or Mike linebacker changed their alignment and aligned on the line of scrimmage. In that case, we may go to a dual rule and squeeze the tackle down on the linebacker, and the running back takes the outside threat.

In our nomenclature, we use three-letter words for three-man slides. "Lou" is a three-man slide to the left side. We use four-letter words for four-man slides and five-letter words for five-man slides. If the left tackle hears the word "Ringo," he knows that is a five-man slide to the right. The terminology is there to assure the offensive linemen that they are all doing the same and correct thing.

That builds confidence, and confidence builds aggression. Being aggressive is the number-one thing an offensive lineman has to be. All the things we do are to reaffirm what we are thinking. That is what communication is. Make sure the system is simple to use and makes sense.

In this formation, we align in a 2x2 tight end set to the right (Diagram #11). The Will linebacker aligns on the slot receiver to the left of the formation. The

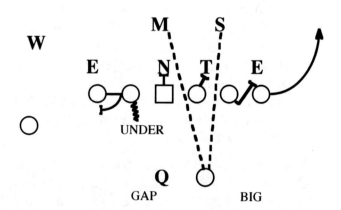

Diagram #11. Slide Under

Will linebacker is out of the box and in coverage. The gap rule says: never slide to nothing. We want to block the defenders that rush. In this case, the nose covers the center so the center does not slide and blocks the nose. The left guard and tackle slide to the left. However, in this example, there is no defender for the guard to slide toward. The left guard gives the center an under call.

The center sets straight back on the nose. The left guard sets under the center, but has a B gap responsibility in the slide. He is in position to help the center with the nose. That allows the center to set slightly to the right and helps him with the inside twist stunt between the nose and 3 technique defender.

Teams will only blitz 40 to 45 percent of the time. That means that 55 percent of the time the defense rushes four defenders in the pass rush. The guard wants the center and tackle to know he can help them with their blocks. We want to build a second level of defense against the pass rusher with the uncovered lineman. The uncovered lineman has to drop and get off the ball when we snap the ball. That way, he can see inside and outside and help if one of the primary blockers get beat or loses his leverage. We pay the linemen to block, not to watch.

If the quarterback is in the shotgun, the right side linemen block their big rules. However, if he gets under the center, they may have to use a dual squeeze technique if one of the linebackers walks up into the line of scrimmage. If the right side blockers have to go to a dual squeeze on their blocks, the tackle gives the back a nonverbal signal that alerts him to the squeeze technique and sends him to the outside on the #3 defender. We use a hand signal rather than a verbal call because it is too hard to hear.

When the back sets up to block the defensive end, about 95 percent of the time, the end breaks down on the back. It is a cardinal rule in the NFL that you are not supposed to block a defensive end with a back. When the back goes to take on the defensive end, the defensive end thinks it may be a screen and does not rush. That is why we do not mind calling this technique occasionally. You can use it to set up the screen if the defensive lineman thinks it is a ploy by the back.

The next defense is an under front with the Will linebacker outside as a threat to rush the passer (Diagram #12). The tackles can see the perimeter better than the center. If the tackle sees the Will linebacker as a pre-rush defender, he makes a call to the center. Any time the defender is outside in open air, we call that a press position. He presses the line of scrimmage and probably has a rush technique. To account for the defensive line, we need a four-man slide. We might the call "Lucy." It can be any four-letter word starting with an L.

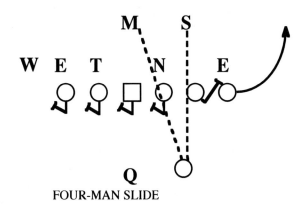

FOUR-MAN SLIDE

Diagram #12. Jet vs. Under

The gap rule is the slide protection. In our slide protection, if a defender does not threaten the gap, the lineman blocks man on. In the diagram, the center's left A gap is not immediately threatened. He posts the nose defender and opens up to the left A gap. The left guard sets on the 3 technique defender, and the tackle sets on the 5 technique defender. If the 5 technique defender takes an inside charge, the tackle steps to the movement, rides the defender, and looks to the outside for the Will linebacker.

If the 3 technique goes inside the guard, he uses the same technique and looks to pick up the 5 technique defender on an inside move. He turns the 3 technique defender over to the center, who posted on the nose and opened into the A gap to pick up the slanting 3 technique. Each offensive lineman protects his gap. He is not blocking a man; he is blocking a gap. If the offensive lineman does not have to slide to protect his gap, he holds his space.

The right guard can set on the outside number of the nose because the center posts up the nose before he goes to his slide technique. When we slide protect, we do not turn the shoulders into the gap. I want the linemen to be square. If the blocker turns into the gap, he opens the gate for the slanting defender coming into the gap. If the lineman is at the beginning of the slide, he cannot pass off a twist game if he turns inside. The defensive end and nose may run a T-E game. The guard and tackle must pass off those defenders. If the guard is not square to the line of scrimmage, he cannot pass off that stunt.

That is the reason I do not call the slide protection a turn protection. In my mind, turn protection means you turn in your technique. We are not turning. We slide to a gap with our shoulders square.

Also on six-man protection, we scan the defense with the back. The reason is the quarterback can only read a dual read to one side of the defense. It is difficult for a quarterback to have a dual responsibility on both sides of the defense. He is throwing hot off the Mike and Sam defenders. If they bring someone from the slot receiver side, it is an unconventional blitz. The back can scan the defense and picks him up.

In the odd front defense, the offensive line has to define who the defenders are in the defense (Diagram #13). There are three down linemen, three linebackers, and five defenders in the secondary. The offensive line is responsible for the four down linemen and the Will linebacker. The center designates the Mike linebacker as the linebacker over the tight end. That means the offensive linemen block the three down linemen and the Buck and Will linebackers. The back reads the Mike linebacker to the strong safety. We designate the strong safety as the Sam linebacker in this protection scheme.

We know the linebacker to the outside is the Will linebacker. He is the most dangerous man. They cannot bring the nickel back out of the secondary unless the linebacker gets into coverage on the slot receiver. In the defensive alignment, we man block the defender and do not slide. That keeps the integrity of the pocket. We want to make the pocket firm whenever possible. That allows the quarterback to step up in the pocket and throw the ball. If the defense can collapse the pocket, the quarterback has to throw going backward.

The five-man protection was our number-one pass protection last year. Many coaches are leery of a five-man protection. I like it because the passes are tempo throws. If the quarterback holds the ball with a five-man protection, you will have to pack the U-Haul. Everything is a tempo throw, and you release five receivers.

We call our five-man protection "gone" because everyone is gone. In the protection, we have zero extra blockers in the scheme. The quarterback takes a pocket drop, which is a five-step, seven-yard deep drop. The guard and tackle to both sides of the protection block a dual rule. The center's responsibility is man. The center's rule is to count for the third defender away from the directional call. In a gone right protection, the center has the #3 defender to the left. We want to block the five MDMs, left to right in the box.

We do not want to be dual on both sides of the protection. We hope the center can take the dual protection out of one side or the other. The preference is the left side. If he cannot take the dual out, the guards and tackles block the two most dangerous defenders to their side from the 0 declaration.

The formation is a two tight end empty set. The protection is gone left (Diagram #14). The down defenders are in an over front to the formation side. The Sam linebacker is in the box aligned outside the formation side tight end. The first thing the center has to do is find the five most dangerous defenders from the right to the left. The defense has the Sam linebacker aligned on air outside the right tight end. The tackle gives his press call to the center. The center gives a Roy call to the offensive line. That

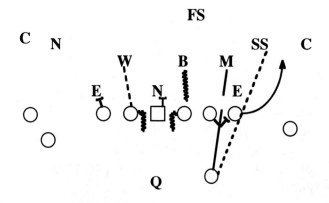

Diagram #13. Jet vs. Odd Front

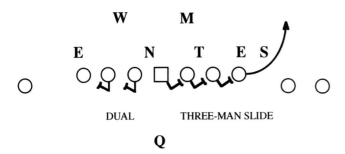

DUAL   THREE-MAN SLIDE

Diagram #14. Gone Left

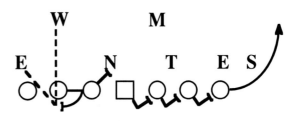

Diagram #16. Gone Left MDM

tells the right side they are in a three-man slide protection. That means the right side is out of dual and into gap protection.

For the quarterback to throw hot, the defense must bring both the Mike and Sam linebackers off the right side. The left side blocks the dual call on the nose and defensive end. However, if the Mike linebacker walked up into the A gap, then the center checks the protection and calls "Ringo" (Diagram #15). That puts us in a five-man slide to the right and releases the right defensive end. His alignment puts him further away from the quarterback.

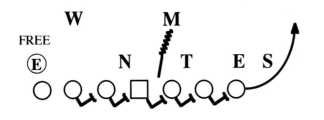

FIVE-MAN SLIDE

Diagram #15. Gone Left Mike Blitz

When we call the gone protection, it is always good to have the tight end set to the directional side of the protection. The alignment of the tight end to that side puts the defensive end farther away from the quarterback. We protect the short edge of the front.

I want to cover one last thing about the dual side of the protection (Diagram #16). The tackle sets on the defensive end and blocks him. However, if the Will linebacker walks up into the backside B gap, the tackle block him and releases the defensive end. He blocks the MDM. However, if the tackle sets on the defensive end and the Will linebacker blitzes from depth, he does not try to come off the defensive end and block the Will linebacker. If a lineman tries to block two defenders in the NFL, he blocks neither of them.

In this protection, it does not matter whether you go strong or weak, or left or right, as long as two things happen. The first thing is the offensive line is in sync on who they are blocking, and the quarterback is in sync with who they are blocking.

As long as the line leaves one defender for the quarterback, and he know which one that is, you are fine. The problem is when the quarterback does not know who is coming hot and the defense destroys him. As long as the offensive line and quarterback work together, the worst thing that can happen is the quarterback throws the ball away. In our case, he throws the ball up for Calvin, and he goes and gets it.

The thing about gone protection is the formations we use. We spread the defense with our formation so they have to tell you what they are doing before you snap the ball. If you are in a two-back offense, the defense can disguise the coverage. When they are five receivers spread all over the field, the disguise is not so good.

I want to show you some drills we do. The first drill is a quick set drill. You can do it two different ways. You can use a bag holder or a live blocker using his shoulder. We drill the movement from head-up, inside, and outside. We work on quick set, hand placement, and stab. All we do is set and punch. When the bag holder moves to the inside, the blocker wants to try to get in front of him on the set. The blocker gives a tiny bit of ground so he can get to the junction point on the defender before the defender can punch him.

If the blocker steps laterally and the defender hits him before he gets to the junction point, he opens up. He has to strike with balance, which means he has to beat the defender to the junction point and punch before the defender.

The next part of the drill we teach with a live player using the shoulder technique (Diagram #17). The blocker aligns on the line and the partner aligns at an angle perpendicular to him on his shoulder. The point of the defender's shoulder points toward the blocker. The blocker quick sets and punches the defender in the shoulder. The defender squares to the line and begins to hand fight and move on the blocker. The blocker hand fights and mirrors the defender's movement. He stays in front of him and works his punch and hand placement against the defender. The defender actively fights his hands and tries to get by the blocker.

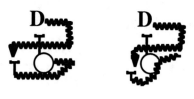

COACH

Diagram #17. Quick Set Finish

The next drill is a simple wave drill. We work all five positions at the same time. The right side players work with their right foot back, and the left side works with their left foot back. The center alternates his footwork with the right foot back and then the left foot back. They work on a 45-degree angle and react off the coach's hand movement. We want the shoulders square with the butt down. We work to keep the feet moving and outside the shoulders. We want to relax the upper body with no wasted motion. We move the linemen back and forth, up and back, changing directions. We work each rep about 10 seconds.

We do a wave drill called angle drill (Diagram #18). I set up five cones in the shape of right angles. The cones are three yards apart. One set of three cones is for the right side linemen, and the other set is for the left side linemen. I work them one at a time. The lineman starts at the middle cone and reacts to the coach's hand movement. He works laterally between the front two cones and at an angle to the back cone. He moves outside, inside,

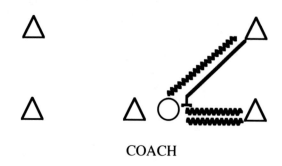

COACH

Diagram #18. Angle Drill

and at a 45-degree angle up and back on the coach's signal. After the left side players go, the right side players do the same drill.

We work the same type of cone shuffle drill with the five cones in a vertical line. The cones are two yards apart. The lineman starts at the first cone and works his feet, moving laterally around each cone. He works right of the cone, changes direction, shuffles to the left side of the next cone, and repeats the movement through the five cones. When they finish going forward, we turn them around, and they do the same thing backward. This is harder because they want to look down and find the cones.

We want the same posture and foot movement. They should see the cones using their peripheral vision. As they work back in their 45-degree movement, they want to keep their shoulders as square to the line as they can.

The dance drill is a position-specific conditioning drill (Diagram #19). This drill is trying to get them comfortable in an unnatural position. We put the left side on one side of the line and the right side on the other side. This is a mirror drill, using weights, sandbags, medicine ball, and other apparatus. If one player takes a short step, the other player mirrors it. With each step, the player punches his hands. In his hands are weight plates, sandbags,

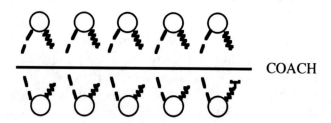

Diagram #19. Dance Drill

or some other weighted apparatus. They step and punch so that the lower body and upper body work independent of each other.

The coach calls out the movement he wants. He may say, "Outside foot set," or "Inside foot post." If the player takes the outside footstep, he has to take a second step to balance. The first step is to post, and the second step is to balance. They take the steps, and the coach makes them hold their position. They work 15 to 20 seconds per repetition. When they have to hold their position, it burns their thighs as you would not believe. It is an unnatural position to try to hold. It is a simple drill, but it works on the steps and techniques, and builds strength in the quads. We do four sets of 15 repetitions. After two sets, they switch sides.

The next drill is a push/pull drill. In this drill, the offensive player does not use his hands. The defensive player gets a grip on the offensive player's jersey. On the command, the defensive player begins to push the offensive player back or pull him forward. He moves him side to side and tries to jerk him off balance. This is a lower body balance drill. The offensive blocker wants to learn how to use his hips, ankles, and knees to maintain his balance. If you are not in jerseys, you can put one hand behind the neck and one hand on the shoulder and do the same thing.

To work on our 45-degree angle step, we do a punch down the line drill (Diagram #20). The blocker aligns on the line of scrimmage. We place a line of bag holders at a 45-degree angle off the line. We have five bag holders in the line. The blocker sets and punches each bag, moving out at a 45-degree angle. They move out on the line of dummies and return to the start point, doing the same thing.

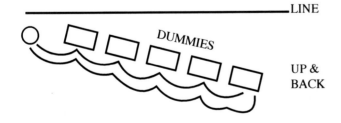

Diagram #20. Punch Down the Line

In this drill, the defensive players go at the pace of the offensive players. When you do this drill, never sacrifice technique for speed. Habits, good or bad, are hard to break. You want to build good habits. If they do not do it right, you are wasting your time. Slow the drill down until they get it.

We film all these drills. At the end of spring workout sessions in about four weeks, we do the same drills and film them. We compare the two films and see what type of improvement they made. You have to change your drills. You cannot do the same drills every day. You need to change up the muscle groupings the linemen use in a drill.

We work the strike drills with medicine balls and sandbags. We do the medicine ball drill between two players. They work their foot movement while punching the medicine ball between them. They throw it back and forth in a punching movement. One partner can throw the ball to the other player, and he can punch the ball back using his stab punch. The sandbag punch drills are the same movements we did in the dance drill. They move their feet out and back while simulating the punch with the sandbag. When we do the sandbag drill, we try to develop the muscle in the upward motion of the punch. At the same time, we work on the shoulders and quads in this drill.

In the mirror drill, we work the offensive blocker staying in front of the rabbit. He mirrors the movement of the rabbit while keeping his posture and footwork going. After five seconds, I call time. The rabbit drops out, and a fresh rabbit enters the drill. The offensive lineman does not change. He continues mirroring the movement of the new rabbit. We work the rabbits for five seconds and the linemen for 15 seconds.

The coach stands behind the offensive lineman and coaches his technique. The word you do not want to use is "don't." They hear the mistake and not the "don't." You say, "Don't lunge," and they lunge.

The last drill is the down back drill (Diagram #21). You need no apparatus. All you need is two lines five yards apart. I teach four basic run steps. Everything we do in the run game has one of those steps. The first step is a basic drive block step. He gets his hips, knees, and ankles in line. We want him to get his knees over his toes and do that for five yards. He uses short, choppy steps as if he were

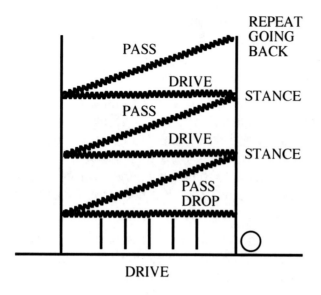

Diagram #21. Down Back

drive blocking. We want him to use perfect form and go as fast as he can. When he hits the five-yard line, he kick slides at a 45-degree angle back to the start line. He gets down in a stance and does it again. We work three sets at the start. We want to work up with our endurance until we work across the field and back.

When he gets to the other end, he repeats the drill, going back the other direction. This puts him in the reverse foot position as he was on the way down.

He starts the second groups of steps with a lateral and drive step movement on the double-team block. He takes a lateral step with his inside foot and repeats the drive block steps for five yards. When he reaches the line, he turns around and does an inside post step at a 45-degree angle back to the line. He repeats the exercise through three repetitions.

The next step is an angle step we use in down blocking. On this step, we start at a 45-degree angle, blocking down. We use the drive block steps on an angle. When he reaches the cone, he faces the other directions, does the 45-degree post step to the next line and repeats.

The last step movement is pulling. The lineman faces down the line, pulls, and runs down the line. He turns and does the post angle step back to the line and repeats the pull movement. We do the four run blocking steps and alternate them with a pass set step.

If I had total control on the conditioning test for offensive linemen, I would make them do down and back across the field four times. That is 100 yards four times. If he can do that, he is in shape to play offensive line. When we start to do this, we go three times over and three times back. We increase the progressions until we work across the field and back.

You must train the linemen and take pride in what you are doing. The offensive line is the hardest position to play, and you will never master it.

ABOUT THE AUTHOR

George Yarno enters his third season as Detroit's offensive line coach. Prior to joining the Lions' coaching staff, Yarno spent the 2008 season as the assistant offensive line coach with Tampa Bay after spending 17 years at the college level, working with the offensive line.

From 2003 to 2007, Yarno worked at his alma mater, Washington State University, in his second stint as the school's offensive line coach. During the 2003 season, he guided All-Pac-10 selections. Yarno began his coaching career with the Cougars from 1991 to 1994.

Over the course of his 17-year college coaching career, Yarno served as an offensive line coach at both Louisiana State University (2001–2002), helping the team win an SEC title (2001) and at Arizona State (2000). Yarno also served as an assistant head coach/offensive line coach at Houston (1998–1999) and as an offensive coordinator/offensive line coach at Idaho (1995–1997).

Prior to coaching, Yarno was a two-time Pac 10 conference honoree as a defensive lineman at Washington State (1975–1979). In 1979, he signed as a free agent with Tampa Bay, where he played for five years (1979–1983). Yarno later joined the Denver Gold of the upstart USFL (1984–1985) before returning to the Buccaneers (1985–1987). Yarno finished out his NFL playing career with Atlanta (1988), Houston (1989) and Green Bay (1990).

Born August 12, 1957, Yarno and his wife, Cindy, have three children, Josh, Adrianne, and George.

About the Editor

Earl Browning is a native of Logan, West Virginia. He currently serves as president of Telecoach, Inc.—an organization that conducts the Nike Coach of the Year Clinics (www.nikecoyfootball.com) and produces the annual *Coach of the Year Clinics Football Manuals* and *Clinic Notes*. A 1958 graduate of Marshall University, he earned his M.Ed. and Rank I education certification from the University of Louisville. From 1958 to 1975, he coached football at various Louisville-area high schools. Among the honors he has been accorded are his appointments to the National Football Foundation and to the College Hall of Fame Advisory Committee on moving the museum to South Bend, Indiana. He was named to the Greater Louisville Football Coaches Association Hall of Legends in 1998. From 1992 to 2010, he served as a radio and television color analyst for Kentucky high school football games, including the Kentucky High School Athletic Association State Championship games.